Twelve Wisdom Steps
Unifying Principles of the
12 Steps of A.A. Found in
the Wisdom Traditions

by

Rev. Dr. Andrea Travers

DORRANCE PUBLISHING CO., INC.
PITTSBURGH, PENNSYLVANIA 15222

This compendium of work is dedicated to all the saints, sages, wisdom teachers, and way-showers who have inspired and guided me to see this vision of universality take form as Twelve Wisdom Steps.

The contents of this work, including, but not limited to, the accuracy of events, people, and places depicted; opinions expressed; permission to use previously published materials included; and any advice given or actions advocated are solely the responsibility of the author, who assumes all liability for said work and indemnifies the publisher against any claims stemming from publication of the work.

Dorrance Publishing Co., Inc.
701 Smithfield Street
Pittsburgh, PA 15222
Visit our website at www.dorrancebookstore.com

ISBN: 978-1-4349-1228-2
eISBN: 978-1-4349-3940-1

Twelve Wisdom Steps

The Unifying Principles of the 12 Steps of A.A. Found in the Wisdom Traditions

Rev. Dr. Andrea Travers

Contents

Chapter One
Introduction

Statistics inform us that over two million people in at least 170 countries are attending A.A. (Alcoholics Anonymous) meetings, and this number does not include the millions who are attending N.A. (Narcotics Anonymous), O.A. (Overeaters Anonymous), C.A. (Cocaine Anonymous); D.D. (Dual Diagnosis Anonymous); CodA (Co-dependents Anonymous); S.L.A. (Sex and Love Anonymous); M.A. (Marijuana Anonymous); D.A. (Debtors Anonymous); Nicotine Anonymous; S.A. (Sex Addicts Anonymous) and the other lesser known applications of the Twelve Step model to various addictions and compulsions. Most people are aware the Twelve Step model is grounded in practices, which can be linked to many religious traditions: honesty, taking an inventory, restitution, prayer and meditation, and service.

As I began working intimately with this model at Hazelden, whose treatment is based on the Minnesota Model that incorporates the Twelve Step program, I became convinced that recovery from addiction was not just attributable to psychotropic medications, psychodynamic therapy or regular attendance at Twelve Step meetings; something else was at play, causing a substantive ego shift. As I continued to work with clients from all faith traditions, I found myself in the position of trying to help them translate the principles and practices of the Twelve Steps into their own religious context of prayer, principles, and practices. This led me to believe there must be universal principles that undergird all the religions and faith traditions; and if so, at a time in our world when we are seeking to better understand each other and find common ground on which to relate, we may need to look no further than to our common universal beliefs and practices.

This, of course, requires that we set our own traditional and cultural lenses aside and open ourselves to merging what we know with a new understanding of shared principles. Because these principles are held sacred by so many cultures, and practiced throughout most of the world, we begin to realize we live in a world of common-unity. Over time, this realization can become so real, so personal, and so integrated into our belief system that we will act from an unprecedented understanding that we are one, universal species on the planet who share common ground despite the richness of our diversity. Our moral imperative, then, is to seek communion with one another while appreciating the abundant differentiation.

This body of work is the culmination of my search to find common unity among the eight wisdom traditions by identifying each of the Twelve Step principles in Buddhism, Christianity, Cosmology, Hinduism, Islam, Judaism, Native American Spirituality, and Taoism. There are three major components:

1) An interactive internet site featuring a *mandala*, which interconnects the Twelve Steps with each of the wisdom traditions, allowing the user to traverse across the steps and through the traditions with ease (www.12wisdomsteps.com).
2) A Spiritual Practices and Facilitator's guide, which accompanies the website. It features spiritual practices from all the wisdom traditions organized by each of the twelve principles that undergird the Twelve Steps with suggestions to begin a daily spiritual practice. It also includes introspective questions related to each step, which can be used in group process facilitation.
    1. Honesty
    2. Hope
    3. Faith

     4. Courage
     5. Integrity
     6. Willingness
     7. Humility
     8. Love
     9. Justice
    10. Perseverance
    11. Spirituality
    12. Service

3) This book is the third component, which is a chronicle of the journey from the inception of the idea to a retrospective reflection.

Chapter Two describes the developmental stages of the concept, the creation of the mandala, the development of the inter-linking architecture required for the website to allow the user to traverse back and forth from each of the Twelve Steps and eight wisdom traditions (ninety-six connecting points with open connectivity).

Chapter Three defines the Twelve Steps; explains how they are a design for living one's life, illustrates how they are a spiritually transformative process; incorporates research data confirming their efficacy; and provides the history and origin of the Twelve Steps program as a social movement in this country.

Chapter Four introduces the wisdom traditions and summarizes the sacred texts cited.

Chapter Five is the compendium of research compiled by relating each of the principles of the Twelve Steps to those found in each of the eight wisdom traditions: Buddhism, Christianity, Cosmology, Hinduism, Islam, Judaism, Native American Spirituality, and Taoism.

Chapter Six is a mountaintop retrospective view of the journey from the larger context of my life. It was an invaluable opportunity to discover how this body of work is an affirmation of my strongest basic beliefs relating to universal ideas, thought, the creative power which is the universe and God and how we are active participators in the process of creation.

Goals and Objectives

My goal is for the www.12wisdomsteps.com website to carry you across the traditional boundaries of religion, history, and spirituality, merging what you know with a newfound understanding that despite the cloak of diversity in its many colors, there are shared unifying principles in all the wisdom traditions. Because these principles are commonly shared, held sacred by most, and practiced by many throughout the world, we begin to realize we live in a world of common-unity. Over time, this realization can become so real, so personal, and so integrated into our belief system that we will act from an unprecedented understanding that we are one, universal species on the planet who share common ground despite the richness of our diversity. Our moral imperative is to seek communion with one another while appreciating the abundant differentiation.

Chapter Two

The Journey

The original idea for this website was born ten years ago when I worked as a Men's Addiction Counselor and Clinical Supervisor at Hazelden Springbrook, a nationally recognized treatment center for chemical dependence. The treatment model used since their inception is based on the Minnesota Model, which integrates the Twelve Steps of A.A. with cognitive-behavioral and psychodynamic treatment methods.

The first thing I learned about this model is its efficacy when the individual is "honest, open, and willing," and in the words of William James, a pioneering America psychologist, philosopher, and physician, the result is a spiritual experience or conversion. Bill Wilson (Bill W.), who founded A.A., further described it in the following words:

> "…when they talk about a spiritual experience…they mean a certain quality of personality change which, in their belief, could not have occurred without the help and presence of the creative spirit of the universe…. I know scarcely an A.A. member of more than a year's standing who still thinks his transformation is wholly a psychological phenomenon based entirely upon his own normal resources. Almost every one of our members will tell you

that, while he may not go along with a clergyman's concept of God, he has developed one of his own on which he can positively depend, one that works for him. We A.A.'s are quite indifferent to what people may call this spiritual experience of ours. But, to us, it looks very much like conversion...."(Wilson 1944).

As I continued to work with this model and met more "recovering" alcoholics and addicts, I was convinced the results were not just attributable to psychotropic medicines, psychodynamic therapy, or regular attendance at Twelve-Step meetings; something else was at play, which caused a substantive ego shift. Hence, my eagerness grew into an avid curiosity to learn what caused the shift and how it could be replicated with some degree of reliability. According to Bill W., "About half of the A.A. members were agnostics or atheists, which dispels the notion that we are only effective with the religiously susceptible" (Wilson 1944).

At this time, it became apparent to me in working with groups of eight to ten residential patients who participated in daily groups from one to three months, that most patients had difficulty integrating the spiritual components of the program. Because the treatment model is based on the Twelve Step principles, patients were grappling with the spiritual concepts of honesty, willingness, faith, surrender, hope, and humility on a fairly consistent basis. Their difficulties ranged anywhere from having no religious upbringing, rejection of their childhood religion, skepticism, or an inability to understand these principles in their own faith traditions. Because of its reputation, Hazelden draws clients from many diverse backgrounds. At one time, my home group included: a Southern Baptist, an African American atheist, a Sikh, an Orthodox Jew, a scientist, and an agnostic. A blend of religious viewpoints was frequently the norm.

As a graduate of rhetorical communication, I found my personal and professional challenge was one of keen listening and attempting to translate the fundamental principles of the Twelve Steps into concepts and language that each patient could understand within their own experiential context. My ultimate goal went a step further: to create a thirst for spirituality (or God as they understood Him/Her/It).

This goal resulted in stretching my borders of understanding far beyond what I could have imagined. I was convinced the fundamental principles of the Twelve Steps were woven through the major faith traditions. In studying and working in the field of human behavior, we learn that rather than being "terminally unique," we are all much the same; sharing similar needs, wants, desires, and longing for answers to the same existential questions. This desire to discover a universally shared truth led me to One Spirit interfaith seminary in New York, where I spent two years studying the eight wisdom traditions. This experience not only confirmed my conviction of the existence of shared unifying principles across religious traditions, it enriched my understanding of the traditions with metaphorical texts, melodious chants and prayers, and culturally vibrant rituals. And, as I had hoped, my ability to translate the language of the Twelve Steps through other religious lens was enhanced and ultimately became a very rewarding experience.

My next goal was grounded in a desire to systemize these unifying principles, allowing anyone to easily view them through the lens of any one of the wisdom traditions. I began by documenting the principles, texts, and spiritual practices from each wisdom tradition into matrices organized in MS Excel spreadsheets.

Figure 1. Sample of a partial matrix worksheet organized in Excel to collect findings for each of the Twelve Steps by wisdom tradition. Matrix files were developed for principles, texts, practices, and resources. The **example below is** displayed not for content, but to illustrate **the** data collection **technique.**

In time, a vision of a mandala (the universal symbol of unity) emerged as a visual illustration that would be the portal to accessing the interconnections of the principles and wisdom traditions—either through the steps or through each of the traditions. The photo below is my first rough draft on poster board, which hung on the back of the closet door in the guest room. As I began to envision the organizational structure of the mandala, this became the prototype – visual, literal, and textual.

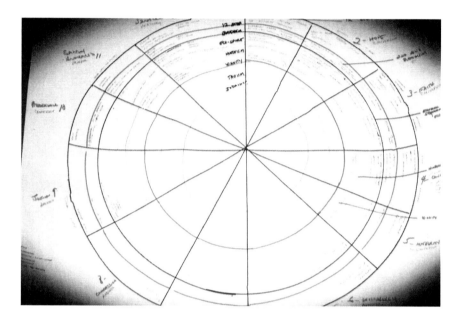

Figure 2. Photo of first prototype of Twelve Step and Wisdom Tradition mandala.

The next stage was to identify an existing mandala structure that could provide the integration and interconnectivity of the Twelve Steps and eight wisdom traditions. I found the Rose mandala design from the Cathedral of Leon in Northern Spain, which has two essential structural components: a series of circular rings and a group of inner petals. At first, I envisioned the rings representing each of the Twelve Steps and the petals intersecting them to provide seventy-two portals (Twelve Steps by eight traditions). This image was later adapted with the circles moving to the outside to identify the steps and the enlarged petals containing the images and links to the wisdom traditions.

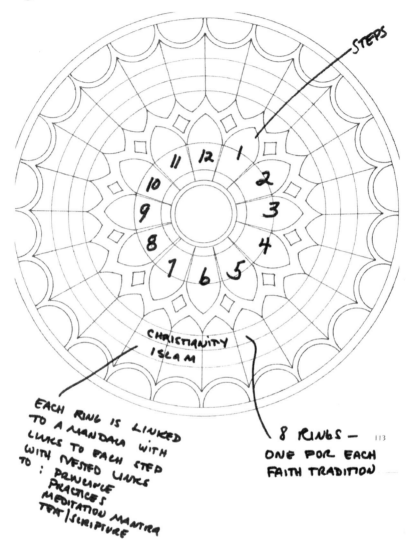

Figure 3. Prototype of mandala based on Rose Mandala from the Cathedral of Leon in Northern Spain, which was later adapted for www.12wisdomsteps.com.

The next step was to find a web architect who could share my vision and develop the intricate, interconnected, linking architecture, which would allow the user to traverse across the steps and through the traditions with ease. I am grateful to have found Andrea Drury at Rareheron Web Design who had both the vision and expertise to build the site and guide me through its technological development. She complemented our efforts with Kayo Parsons-Korn, whose artistry gifted the site with colors and images, which depict the richness of the ages.

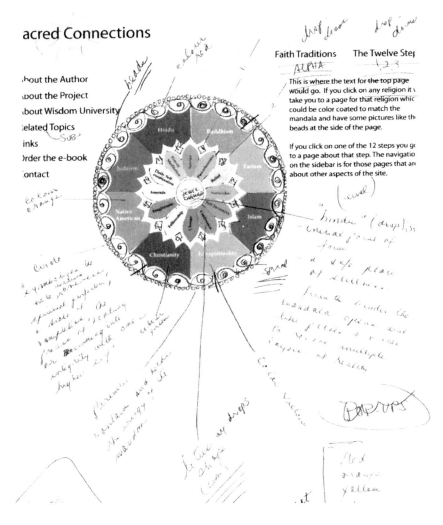

Figure 4. Adaptation from Rose mandala (see Figure 3)

Once the website was completed in July 2009 (which was one-and-a-half year after the research was started and seven months after the web design was initiated), the site was beta-tested in order to obtain feedback about the content and ease of use and access. The following questionnaire with a link to the website was emailed to a pool of fifty reviewers, who included counselors, counselors in recovery, ministers, acquaintances with no connection to addiction/recovery/Twelve Steps, acquaintances in recovery and family with no addiction/recovery connections.

Unifying Principles of the Twelve Steps in the Wisdom Traditions—Website Beta Review Questionnaire

1. Does the Home page adequately explain the **purpose** of the website?

   ☐Yes ☐No   If you checked NO, please indicate missing information

2. Do the **instructions and overall design** make it easy to use?

   ☐Yes ☐No   If you checked NO, what would help make it easier?

3. Are you able to easily **migrate** through the various Wisdom traditions and Twelve-Steps?

   ☐Yes ☐No   If you checked NO, please describe the barrier/difficulty

4. Are the **resources** easy to locate, and relevant to your interests?

   ☐Yes ☐No   If you checked NO, what else would you like to see included?

5. Does the information in the Wisdom traditions clearly mirror the **unifying spiritual principles** as defined by the Twelve Steps?

   ☐Yes ☐No   If you checked NO, what would promote more clarity?

6. Does the home page **mandala** depict the integration of the Twelve Steps and the Wisdom traditions?

☐Yes   ☐No   If you checked NO, what could be
                added to better achieve this goal?

_____

_____

7. Is this website a **resource** you could see yourself using
    in the future?

    ☐Yes   ☐No   If you checked YES, how do you see it
                    being a resource?

8. As a resource, in which area would this website be
    more **useful** to you?

    ☐Wisdom Tradition   ☐Twelve Steps   Please explain:

_____

_____

9. If you were given the opportunity to contribute any
    ONE thing to the website, what would it be?

_____

_____

10. Other comments: _____

_____

Demographic profile:

Are you in recovery?	☐Yes	☐No
Are you familiar with the Twelve- Steps?	☐Yes	☐No
Have you studied the Wisdom Traditions?	☐Yes	☐No
Is this an aspect of spirituality, which interests you?	☐Yes	☐No
If you had this application on your desktop, would you use it?	☐Yes	☐No

How do you rate your web browsing skills?

      ☐Inexperienced   ☐Competent   ☐Proficient

Figure 5. Questionnaire sent to beta-site reviewers, July 2009.

Chapter Three

What Are the Twelve Steps?

"Clergymen of all denominations say they are good religion...." (Wilson 1944)

The Twelve Steps have often been described as a design or a blueprint for living. They have been adapted by hundreds of groups to address most obsessive/compulsive disorders, including gambling, sex, video games, food, pornography, alcohol, and drugs. Current estimates indicate over two million people actively attend Twelve-Step meetings and the number of groups worldwide exceeds 100,000. Many consider it to be the most successful social movement in the 21st century.

The Steps are based on principles which, when practiced regularly, become a daily discipline; the result is personal growth. People become more honest with themselves and others, they shift from negativism to positivism, they become less ego-centered and more other-centered, they recognize their character flaws and work to overcome them, they become accountable for themselves and their actions, they make restitution when harm has been done, they inventory their actions daily, they practice meditation and prayer to build a relationship with God (or a Higher Power), and they perform service or volunteer work regularly.

Step One - Admitting Defeat☐

We admitted we were powerless over our addiction(s), that our lives had become unmanageable.

Principle: Honesty

The step is a statement of the problem; an admission of the force in our lives over which we are powerless, causing our lives to become unmanageable. The underlying principle is **honesty,** which allows one to break through the denial and recognize there is a problem.

Step Two - Return to Sanity☐

Came to believe that a Power greater than ourselves could restore us to sanity.

Principle: Hope

This step states there is a solution to the problem and it is spiritual in nature. It offers **hope** and requires one to begin to look inside oneself for the solution. The promise is to be restored to a state of rational thinking or sanity.

Step Three—Trust☐

Made a decision to turn our will and our lives over to the care of God as we understood Him.

Principle: Faith

This is an action step, which requires making a decision to do something different in search of finding a solution. It requires developing **faith** in something other than our own ability to control. It is the beginning of surrender to a Higher Power.

Step Four - Looking Within☐

Made a searching and fearless moral inventory of ourselves.

Principle: Courage

This *step* requires individual **courage** to explore one's own history of denial and self-deception. This is accomplished by identifying the barriers that prevent us from progressing spiritually: our resentments, fears, and harm done to relationships with the Divine, self, others, and Earth.

Step Five—Secrets☐

Admitted to God, to ourselves, and to another human being the exact nature of our wrongs.

Principle: Integrity

This step provides an opportunity to re-align oneself with one's values and to accept the duality of *one's* imperfections and one's gifts, talents, and worth. The result is a shift into acting in **integrity** and recognizing when one is not, followed by taking a corrective step.

Step Six - New Ways☐

Were entirely ready to have God remove all these defects of character.

Principle: Willingness

This step involves yet another commitment to change and is characterized by a **willingness** to partner with (God) or one's Higher Power (which may include a sponsor) to work on changing one's self-defeating attitudes, behaviors, and belief system.

Step Seven - Courage to Change☐

Humbly asked Him to remove our shortcomings.

Principle: Humility

This step actually deepens one's faith. It is a **humble** recognition of one's own shortcomings and limitations and a firm commitment to change them in order to increase one's sense of worthiness as an individual and unique reflection of God's image.

Step Eight - Facing the Consequences☐

Made a list of all persons we had harmed, and became willing to make amends to them all.

Principle: Love

This step emerges from one's increased capacity to **love** self and others, which results ultimately from taking responsibility for one's own actions (past, present, and future). When one does this in a thorough and heartfelt manner, one moves from being a victim of circumstances and blaming external causes to taking responsibility for oneself.

Step Nine - Confronting the Past☐

Made direct amends to such people whenever possible, except when to do so would injure them or others.

Principle: Justice

This step is *grounded* in a newly-developed understanding or sense of **justice**. It requires not saying you're sorry (again) for harms done, but actually making amends or paying restitution in kind to those harmed. Once this step is completed, one is finally able to release the shame and guilt from the past and experience a new freedom.

Step Ten—Vigilance☐

Continued to take personal inventory and when we were wrong, promptly admitted it.

Principle: Perseverance

This step requires discipline and **perseverance.** As with any newly developed skill or talent, regular practice and discipline are necessary until it becomes a habit. Remission is possible without vigilance to living the principles of this program. These steps only work if they are practiced daily as a way of life.

Step 11 - Embracing the Mystery☐

Sought through prayer and meditation to improve our conscious contact with God as we understood Him, praying only for knowledge of His will for us and the power to carry that out.

Principle: Spirituality

This step reminds us that our **spirituality** will only emerge from within and grow when we dedicate ourselves to a daily practice of reflection, prayer, and meditation; and in so doing, we will learn to trust a power greater than ourselves to guide us.

Step 12—Awakening☐

Having had a spiritual awakening as the result of these steps, we tried to carry this message to others, and to practice these principles in all our affairs.

Principle: **Service**

This step is based on the principle that we can only keep what we have by giving it away. **Service** to others increases self-worth, engenders inner joy, and changes our focus from self-centeredness to other-centeredness.

The principles (in boldface) underlying these steps are considered in A.A. to be "guides." The principles have been printed in A.A. literature throughout the years, but "the origin of them is unknown."

Adherence to these principles is not a condition of (A.A.) membership; however, its efficacy is dependent on adherence to these principles. Bill W. defined the conversion process:

> "The alcoholic, objecting at first to the spiritual factor, is urged to keep an open mind, meanwhile treating his own A.A. group as a 'power greater than himself.' Under these conditions, the newcomer commences to undergo a personality change at such a rate and of such dimensions that he cannot fully account for it on the basis of self-realization and self-discipline. Not only does his alcoholic obsession disappear, but, also, he finds himself progressively free of fear, resentment, and inferiority. These changes seem to have come about automatically. Hence, he concludes that 'A power greater than himself' must have indeed have been at work. Having come to this point, he begins to form his own concept of God. He then develops confidence in that concept, which grows as he gets proof in everyday life that his new faith actually works, really produces results. This is what A.A.'s are trying to say when they talk about a spiritual experience. They mean a certain quality of personality change which, in their belief, could not have occurred without the help and presence of the creative spirit of the universe" (Wilson 1944)

Twelve Steps - A Design for Living

The Twelve Steps were founded by alcoholics who figured out how to stay sober by helping each other and adopting a set of disciplined practices, which, over time, resulted in a transformation of thinking and behavior. They have been called a design for living, and the practices related to the steps are a way of living.

Substance use, when viewed through the criteria of dependence (or inability to control or stop using despite a history of adverse consequences) affects about 20 percent of the population. Approximately 15 percent of this group receives treatment. Alcoholism alone is responsible for over 200,000 deaths annually in this country, which ranks it third as a cause of mortality (Rieger 1990, 2511-18).

In 1935, Dr. William Silkworth, who treated Bill W. in the Charles B. Towns Hospital in New York, described alcoholism in medical terms as a "compulsion.... This is a pathological craving, this is a disease.... an obsession of the mind that condemns one to drink and an allergy of the body that condemns one to die," (*A.A.Grapevine* May 1951).

In these early days, he believed it was a hopeless disease, but had also witnessed 'psychic changes' that resulted in long-term recovery.

The primary purpose of the Twelve Steps program is to provide mutual help through support groups, which promote abstinence. They are free and easily available; many find sobriety through this method. The preamble of Alcoholics Anonymous best describes its purpose and mission:

"Alcoholics Anonymous is a fellowship of men and women who share their experience, strength, and hope with each other that they may solve their common problem and help others to recover from alcoholism. The only requirement for membership is a desire to stop drinking. There are no dues or fees for A.A. membership; we are self-supporting through our own contributions. A.A. is not allied with any sect, denomination, politics, organization or institution; does not wish to engage in any controversy; neither endorses nor opposes any causes.

Our primary purpose is to stay sober and help other alcoholics to achieve sobriety," (A.A. Grapevine 1947).

A.A. is a fellowship of members with a common experience (and disease) who are seeking recovery (life without dependence on drugs and alcohol). One of the fundamental principles is hope, which comes from new members hearing the stories of how those with sobriety were able to find their way through their suffering to a new life in recovery. There are no requirements; it is a completely voluntary program.

A.A., as with most organizations, has a hierarchical structure. There is a General Service Board, which functions as trustees and oversees the A.A. World Services, Inc., and the A.A. Grapevine Inc. The General Service Office in New York is the clearinghouse for all A.A. information and literature. Anyone can start up an A.A. meeting. Monies contributed voluntarily during meetings pay for rent for the meeting room, literature, and coffee. The *Twelve Steps and Twelve Traditions* provide the guidelines. There are no bylaws or rules.

Meetings are designed to provide support for those whose goal is to maintain abstinence. Newcomers are always welcomed. There are many types of meetings: open meetings for anyone interested; closed meetings for current participants only; speaker meetings; Big Book study groups; Step study groups; discussion groups; smoking and non-smoking meetings; gender specific; and many are dedicated to specific sub-populations such as youth, professional groups, religious groups, newcomers or "old-timers." Meetings are easy to find, usually listed in the Yellow Pages; often held in churches and local meeting halls, and now easily found through Google.

A typical meeting begins with introductions ("My name is _____ and I'm an alcoholic.). There is a reading from the *Big Book* or the *Twelve Steps and Twelve Traditions*. Business announcements are made. The person chairing the meeting introduces a discussion topic and everyone is invited to speak about how it relates to them and their recovery. A basket is passed for voluntary donations. The meeting is often closed with the Serenity prayer and there is ample time for coffee and discussion after the meetings. Over time, people usually identify a "home group" which they attend more frequently and through which they can rely on others knowing them and their story (of their addiction/recovery).

There are several activities that are considered integral to "working a Twelve-Step program:"

- Ongoing contact with one's sponsor (or coach)
- Reading the Big Book of A.A.
- Working the steps (one-at-a-time until completing all twelve)
- Attending meetings
- Completing a daily Tenth Step inventory
- Prayer and meditation

A.A. is designed to be a one-day-at-a-time program, which grew out of the commitment to 'stay sober just for today.' The service aspect of this program is also critical to being successful. It is founded on the Twelfth Step principle which is "You can only keep sobriety by giving it away" – by helping another person find his or her way. This is fundamental to sponsorship (or coaching), which is the foundation of A.A. service work. A Twelfth Step phone call made at any time of the day or night is an alternative to picking up a glass of alcohol or a drug.

Because addiction continues to be an incurable disease, this program is the only universal, no-cost, easily accessible program, which has proven efficacy for those who chose to avail themselves of it – "It works if you work it."

How the Steps work - "It works if you work it"
Alcoholics Anonymous began when Bill W. called Dr. Bob Smith on a rainy night while staying at the Mayflower Hotel in Akron, Ohio, for a business meeting.

"Alone in a strange city, with ten dollars (U.S.) in his pocket and the familiar taste of failure (business) in his mouth, he badly wanted a drink..he found himself slowly drifting toward the bar...; (however,) his long stride took him to the other end of the lobby...and on the side of the (telephone) booth, he noticed a church directory...; if he could help someone else to stop drinking, perhaps he would feel better..... He picked out the name Reverend Walter Tunks.... who was a strong Oxford Grouper who gave him ten names and telephone numbers to find "a drunk to talk with," (Cheeve 2004, 133).

A.A. began when Bill W. and Dr. Bob both carried their message to the third member, Bill D. The message was: Recovery is possible. And that message is still conveyed today, every day, by someone who *has* recovered from alcoholism telling the story of their recovery to someone else who needs to hear it.

"A.A. is a synthetic concept...drawing upon the resources of medicine, psychiatry, religion, and our own experience of drinking and recovery. We have merely streamlined old and proved principles of psychiatry and religion into such forms that the alcoholic will accept them," (Wilson 1944).

The basis of the Twelve Steps comes from the original principles of the Oxford Group, an evangelical movement founded in Great Britain. The core practices are considered to be what is responsible for the conversion of character:

- admission of powerlessness
- taking a daily moral inventory
- restitution for harms done
- service to others
- surrender to a personal God or Higher Power

It is important to remember this program and its steps emerged from the common experiences of people who, out of desperation of not being able to find another way, started to use spiritual principles to guide their lives. And much like many religions, these principles were handed down orally as a record of their own personal experience.

Bill W. had a profound experience in the midst of alcohol withdrawal while on medication in Towns Hospital after he was informed by Dr. Silkworth, who was medical director of Charles B. Towns Hospital, which specialized in the treatment of alcoholism, his case was "hopeless." It was such a phenomenal experience, he questioned whether it was an hallucination or a spiritual awakening. He had been studying William James' book, *Varieties of Religious Experience*, in which he described conversion experiences resulting from one's ability to surrender after periods of great suffering. Ernest Kurtz, in his study of the development of this movement, emphasizes two key influences directly related to Silkworth and James: 1) the sense of hopelessness and 2) the conversion experience (Kurtz 1979, 222).

This experience led Bill W. to begin exploring the Oxford group and its practices, which were based on Christian practices and principles. At the time, Dr. Bob was an active member of the Oxford group in Akron.

In 1955, at a convention, Bill W. finally talked openly about his awakening or conversion experience. In his words, he described it as,

"All at once, I found myself crying out, 'If there is a God, let Him show Himself! I am ready to do anything, anything.'" And he told how his hospital room filled with white light. "I was caught up into an ecstasy for which there are no words to describe. It seemed to me, in the mind's eye, that I was on a mountain and that a wind not of air but of spirit was blowing. And then it burst upon me that I was a free man. Slowly, the ecstasy subsided. I lay on the bed, but now for a time I was in another world, a new world of consciousness. All about me and through me there was a wonderful feeling of Presence, and I thought to myself, *So this is the God of the preachers!* A great peace stole over me and I thought, *No matter how wrong things seem to be, they are all right. Things are all right with God and His world,*" (Wilson 1957).

Immediately following this experience, Dr. Silkworth examined him, assessed him as rational and sane, and determined he had a spiritual experience.

As A.A. spread, many members found the Oxford group principles to be too religious and realized the need for a clear distinction between Oxford, A.A., religion, and spirituality. As they developed the Steps, they were successful in basing them on universal spiritual principles that are inclusive and non-religious, which allow everyone to define their own understanding of their "Higher Power." This, of course, opens up inclusivity across religious boundaries.

The practical application of this spirituality is based on the recognition of one's own limitations. "We are not cured of alcoholism. What we really have is a daily reprieve contingent on the maintenance of our spiritual condition," (Alcoholics Anonymous 1976).

"The spiritual emphasis of the Twelve Step meetings can begin to help the active addict move from the helplessness and hopelessness of addiction to a sense of reawakening of the human spirit. This is the beginning of hope, which can result in dramatic life change if the individual is able to live using the spiritual tools presented in the Twelve Steps," (Seppala 2001).

Spiritual discipline is a key component of all religions and faith traditions, just as it is with the Twelve Steps. "Working the steps...for most members involves action and thought. It is a form of a cognitive behavioral approach that encourages examination of personal behavior through the filter of a Higher Power.... it places the individual's wishes in a secondary position to the spiritual path they have chosen," (Seppala 2001).

Because the founders knew how important it is to understand how the program works, and what the benefits are, they included both "How It Works" and the "Promises" in the Big Book of Alcoholics Anonymous. The Promises read:

> "If we are painstaking about this phase of our development, we will be amazed before we are half way through. We are going to know a new freedom and a new happiness. We will comprehend the meaning of the word

'serenity' and we will know peace. No matter how far down the scale we have gone, we will see how our experience can benefit others. That feeling of uselessness and self-pity will disappear. We will lose interest in selfish things and gain interest in our fellows. Self-seeking will slip away. Our whole attitude and outlook upon life will change. Fear of people and of economic insecurity will leave us. We will intuitively know how to handle situations, which used to baffle us. We will suddenly realize that God is doing for us what we could not do for ourselves. Are these extravagant promises? We think not. They are being fulfilled among us—sometimes quickly, sometimes slowly. They will always materialize if we work for them," (Alcoholics Anonymous 1976).

Twelve Rewards

1. Hope instead of desperation
2. Faith instead of despair
3. Courage instead of fear
4. Peace of mind instead of confusion
5. Self-respect instead of self-contempt
6. Self-confidence instead of helplessness
7. Respect of others instead of pity and contempt
8. Clean conscience instead of guilt
9. Real friendship instead of loneliness
10. Clean pattern of life instead of purposeless existence
11. Love and understanding of our families instead of their doubts and fears
12. Freedom of a happy life instead of the bondage of an obsession

Efficacy of Twelve Step Programs

Today A.A. is an extensive mutual-help organization that spans the globe. There are over two million members in over 170 countries.

U.S. Worldwide

	U.S.	Worldwide
Members	1,187,168	2,066,851
Groups	52,735	104,589

Figure 6. A.A. World Services, 2004

Research is limited due to the anonymity of the program and its members, most of which has been conducted by the A.A. organization itself. 395 members who were followed for eight years in a study that had positive outcomes after the first three years related to:

- Remission for alcohol problem
- Lowers levels of depression
- Higher quality of relationships (Humphreys, Moos and Cohen 1997, 231-8).

In 1998, 3,018 veterans were monitored for one year by Ouimette, Moos, and Finney. Those who were continuing A.A. attendance from nine to twelve months reported:

- More abstinence
- Freedom from substance abuse problems
- Freedom from significant distress and psychiatric problems
- More incidents of employment

The following table illustrates a direct correlation between the frequency of meetings attended per week and abstinence rates.

A.A. Meetings 1st Year	Abstinence 1st Year	Abstinence 8th Year
No A.A. attendance	21%	35%
2-4 meetings/wk.	43%	57%
5+ meetings/wk.	61%	73%

Figure 7. Moos 2006 (Ilgen and Moos 2006, 1758-64).

George E. Valiant, in *The Natural History of Alcoholism,* found that the individuals who gained the most benefit from A.A. attended an average of 300 meetings over an eight-year period (Valiant 1976, 234). The following table illustrates the direct correlation between the duration of time attending meetings and abstinence rates:

No. of Years attended A.A.	No. of Weeks attended A.A.	% Abstinent after 8 years
1st Year	None	35%
	1-16 weeks	43%
	17-32 weeks	56%
	33+ weeks	71%
Years 2 thru 8	None	48%
	1-12 months	33%
	13-48 months	64%
	49+ months	89%

Figure 8. Moos, 2006

An A.A. membership survey conducted by A.A. World Services in 1998 determined the four primary factors resulting in an individual's involvement in A.A.:

1. Accompanied to an A.A. meeting by another A.A. member
2. Introduced to A.A. by a treatment facility
3. Came on their own volition
4. Received encouragement from a family member

Research published by www.Join Together.org, which provides news coverage, resources, and advocacy for the advancement of effective drug and alcohol policy, prevention and treatment, published a research summary on February 2, 2010 entitled, *A.A. Attendance Cuts Drinking and Depression, Study Finds*. The article was originally published in the *Los Angeles Times* on January 28, 2010. It reported that a study conducted by John F. Kelly of Harvard Medical School found that A.A. participants, who attended A.A. meetings, drank less. "Some critics of A.A. have claimed that the organization's emphasis on 'powerlessness' against alcohol use and the need to work on 'character defects' cultivates a pessimistic view, but this suggests the opposite is true. A.A. is a complex social organization with many mechanisms of action that probably differ for different people and change over time. Most treatment programs refer patients to A.A. or similar Twelve-step groups, and now clinicians can tell patients that along with supporting abstinence, attending meetings can help improve their mood."

Origin of the Twelve Steps

The Twelve Steps were founded in this country by Bill W., a former Wall Street broker who, "when alcohol had destroyed both his health and his career, had an epiphany that would change his life and the lives of millions of other alcoholics. Incarcerated for the fourth time at Manhattan's Towns Hospital in 1934, (during which time he studied William James' book the *Varieties of Religious Experience*) Bill W. had a spiritual awakening—a flash of white light, a liberating awareness of God—that led to the founding of Alcoholics Anonymous and Bill's revolutionary Twelve Step program, the successful remedy for alcoholism," (Cheever 2004).

William James' work had a significant impact on Bill W.'s thinking. In combination with his own spiritual experience, he learned that most conversion experiences have a common denominator – a collapse of the ego, which for alcoholics and addicts is most often hopelessness and the despair of being trapped in their addictive patterns.

It is also informative to consider the historical context in which this movement emerged. There were two major schools of thought influencing religions – one theological and the other humanistic. The theological school purported the need for salvation in order to be saved (which is a gift bestowed on one by God). The humanists believed that people can be responsible for their change and in some sense, "save" themselves during their lifetime. During the developing years of A.A., the two schools were represented on one hand by the Calvinists and the other by Ralph Waldo Emerson and the transcendentalists. The rudiments of the Steps actually reflect both schools. A key ingredient is the surrender of the ego to a Higher Power, which is greater than self and a reliance on this Power for guidance, which incorporates a requisite dependence on God. However, because the principles emphasize accountability for one's actions and are action-oriented by nature, they are humanistic in their application.

It is also important to understand the definition of alcoholism, which was somewhat different in the 1930s than it is today. At that time, the description in the *Big Book of Alcoholics Anonymous* was—drinkers who can stop drinking, but who apparently cannot stay stopped. They want to stop getting drunk. They mean to stop getting drunk. They resolve to stop getting drunk. But their experience tells them, time and time and time again, that they *cannot* stop getting drunk. The primary characteristic of those whose lives were disrupted by drinking alcohol to the point they would consider A.A., was they did not understand what was going on within themselves, their inability to control their actions and their lives. Most individuals were confused to the point of being terrified because they did not understand what was happening to them.

Bill W., inspired by a friend (Rowland H.) who was able to quit drinking by attending meetings of the Oxford Group, also began attending these meetings. The group was an evangelical society founded in Britain, which produced some degree of success with alcoholics. Rowland was Wilson's connection to both Carl Jung and the Oxford Group. Rowland H. was treated by the famous psychiatrist, Carl Jung, in Zurich. His condition became hopeless which led Jung to the conclusion that 'the only possible cure was a spiritual experience.' He recommended that Rowland join the Oxford group, a Christian evangelical movement. There, he met Ebby Thacher and learned how he had a conversion experience and was able to stop drinking. In 1961, Bill W. wrote Carl Jung to inform him that his treatment of Rowland and recommendation to the Oxford Movement "was to become the first link in the chain of events that led to the founding of Alcoholics Anonymous," (Cheever 2004).

Five tenets of the Oxford movement became the basis of five of the A.A. Twelve Steps: taking a moral inventory, admitting to another the harms done, making amends and restitution, prayer/meditation, and being of service to others. The underlying and most significant discovery was the need to combine spiritual principles with practical actions.

With all due respect to A.A., it is necessary to pause and gain a deeper understanding of the Oxford Group's principles, for without them, there undoubtedly would not be an A.A. movement. A Lutheran Minister, Frank Buchman, who moved from Philadelphia to attend Oxford University, founded the Oxford Group. He had a personal spiritual transformation and formed a Christian evangelical group, which spread from Europe to India, South Africa, China, Egypt, Switzerland, and the Americas. The group practiced four Absolutes: Purity, Honesty, Unselfishness, and Love. The Absolutes were rejected by A.A. as being too perfectionist. Hence, they also "avoided aggressive evangelism, embraced anonymity, and strove to avoid offending anyone who might need the (Oxford) program," (Kurtz 1979).

There was emphasis on confession of wrongs or "sharing" and a practice of amends "restitution." Problems were sorted out during quiet, meditative time. They also practiced the Five "C's":

confidence, confession, conviction, conversion, and continuance. And, much like A.A., the groups were considered a "fellowship." Oxford groups were attended by well-recognized leaders of the day: Henry Ford, Mae West, Harry Truman, and Joe DiMaggio. Bill W.'s first transcription of the Oxford style steps in A.A. language reads:

1. We admitted we were licked.
2. We got honest with ourselves.
3. We talked it over with another person.
4. We made amends to those we had harmed.
5. We tried to carry this message to others with no thought of reward.
6. We prayed to whatever God we thought there was.

Bill W. attended the Oxford Group meetings for four or five months, before his stay in Town's Hospital. These steps and meetings did not keep him sober at this point in time, but certainly sowed seeds of understanding about spiritual principles, their practical applications, and the need for a movement grounded in service and fellowship.

Once there was a constituency of about 100 recovering alcoholics, Bill W. began writing the principles of sobriety with the intention of publishing them. Each chapter was read at the New York Clinton Street meetinghouse and was also read and edited by Dr. Bob Smith's group in Akron, Ohio. The chapters were also reviewed by the editors of *The New Yorker* and the *New York Daily News,* who recovered through A.A.. While Bill W. was writing, the members of the New York and Akron groups began writing their own stories, which comprised the second half of the *Big Book of Alcoholism Anonymous* – the personal testimonials of their successes. These writings were published in April 1939 as *Alcoholics Anonymous* with an initial press run of about 5,000 books.

Most of the stories in the first edition of *Alcoholics Anonymous* came from the early fellowship of the Akron members. There were twice as many sober in Akron as in New York, and even during the book-writing process, these members had fewer relapses. Dr. Smith, who was the presiding physician for many of these members, focused not on their drinking, but on the spiritual, which is a common thread in their stories. These differentiate from the stories of the New Yorkers, most of whom were proud to be agnostics.

During the next few years, as Bill continued his commitment to the movement, his finances were depleted. He was introduced to philanthropist John D. Rockefeller, Jr., whose family had long supported temperance and prohibition. Rockefeller, Jr. was impressed by the work and its accomplishments and created a fund that disbursed a weekly stipend to Bill W. and Dr. Bob (Smith) for their continued work in A.A. He also assisted Bill W. in setting up a tax-free foundation, which could accept donations for the movement.

A.A. and its principles finally gained notoriety in March 1941 when Jack Alexander published an article in the *Saturday Evening Post*. He traveled with Bill W. to meetings in Pennsylvania, Ohio and Chicago and personally heard the success stories of people whose lives had previously been ravaged by addiction. At that time, the *Post* had over three million subscribers and was able to generate national attention for this movement. As a result, attendance at meetings tripled and it began to support itself. Today there are over two million A.A. members in 150 countries.

One of the major contributions of A.A., which we realize today, is the understanding that addiction is a disease, which requires a holistic approach to recovering – a healing of the mind, body, and spirit.

Chapter Four
The Wisdom Traditions

Most of the Wisdom Traditions evolved during the Axial Age, between 900 and 200 BCE. Karen Armstrong, renowned modern theologian, asks; "Why should we go back to these ancient faiths? Because in this period of history, people worked as hard to find a cure for their spiritual ills as we do today trying to find a cure for cancer…none of them were interested in doctrines or metaphysical beliefs…(at that time) a religion was about behaving in a 'way' that changed you," (Armstrong 2006).

References to the 'way' are made in all the wisdom traditions. The 'way' is not a single path, but all the varied paths, which lead to the same destination. As trekkers on the path, we discover that the 'way' is the path through life. It is our own personal journey of finding meaning, truth, and purpose. And, in time, we also learn there is no final destination in this life – the meaning is the journey.

The fact that the spiritual principles found at the core of the Twelve Steps of A.A. are so easily traceable throughout all the Wisdom Traditions suggests these principles are universal – crossing the boundaries of culture, language, religion, time, political ideologies, and belief systems.

When looking across the spectrum of the Wisdom Traditions, we find seven common spiritual themes:

1. Spirit exists (no matter what it is called).
2. Spirit is found within.
3. Most of us live in a "fallen" or "'illusory" state that creates our sense of separation.
4. There is a "way" or "path" out of this state that results in freedom or liberation.
5. If we follow the "path," we will be "awakened" or "enlightened" and experience the Spirit within.
6. This change will end our spiritual longing.
7. As a result, we will grow in compassion and hear the call to be in service for the good of all sentient beings and for the Earth.

As we filter the Twelve Steps of A.A. through the lenses of the various Wisdom Traditions, we discover that each Tradition provides a path; a guide to follow encased in a language, culture, and history indigenous to their understanding. This can only mean that throughout the past 4,000 years, humans have longed for answers to the same existential questions.

The historical framework of each of these traditions helps us understand that we belong to a much larger whole; this wholeness informs us that things are far more integrated than they seem. The narrowing gap today between quantum physics and spiritual mysticism confirms this ancient belief. Houston Smith, in the *Illustrated World's Religions*, describes this experience as being in the mystery,

> "...knowledge and ignorance advance lockstep. As known unknowns become known, unknown unknowns proliferate; the larger the island of knowledge, the longer the shoreline of wonder. It's like the quantum world. The more we understand its formalism, the stranger that world becomes. Things are more integrated than they seem, they are better than they seem, and they are more mysterious than they seem; this is the vision that the wisdom traditions bequeath us," (Smith 1995).

Because these universal principles are commonly shared, held sacred by most, and practiced by many throughout the world, we begin to realize we live in a world of common unity. Over time, this realization may become so true, so personal, and so integrated into our belief system that we will act from an unprecedented understanding that we are one universal species on the planet, who share common ground. We will have a heightened awareness of the richness of our diversity. Our moral imperative will be to seek communion with one another while appreciating our abundant differentiation.

Summary of Wisdom Texts Cited
Buddhism-

There are a variety of Buddhist scriptures and texts. Some schools of Buddhism venerate certain texts as religious objects in themselves, while others take a more scholastic approach. Buddhist scriptures are written in Pali, Tibetan, Mongolian, Chinese, Sanskrit, and a hybrid Buddhist/Sanskrit.

Buddhism has no single central text that is universally referred to by all traditions. Many find the size and complexity of the Buddhist canons as barriers to the wider understanding of Buddhist philosophy. However, some scholars have referred to the *Vinaya Pitaka* and the first four *Nikayas* of the *Sutra Pitaka* as the common core of all Buddhist traditions. Mahayana considers these merely a preliminary and not a core teaching. Tibetan Buddhists have not translated most of the *Agamas*, though theoretically, they recognize them, and they play no part in the religious life of either clergy or laity in China and Japan (Harvey 1990).

The followers of Theravada Buddhism take the scriptures known as the *Pali Canon* as definitive and authoritative, while the followers of Mahayana Buddhism base their faith and philosophy primarily on the Mahayana *Sutras* and their own *Vinaya*. The *Pali Sutras*, along with other closely related scriptures, are known to the other schools as the *Agamas*.

Over the years, various attempts have been made to synthesize a single Buddhist text that can encompass all of the major principles of Buddhism. In the Theravada tradition, condensed "study texts" were created that combined popular or influential scriptures into single volumes that could be studied by novice monks. Later, in Sri Lanka, the *Dhammapada* was championed as a unifying scripture.

Dwight Goddard collected a sample of Buddhist scriptures, with the emphasis on Zen, along with other classics of Eastern philosophy, such as the *Tao Te Ching*, into his 'Buddhist Bible' in the 1920s. More recently, Dr. Babasaheb Ambedkar attempted to create a single, combined document of Buddhist principles in *The Buddha and His Dhamma*. Other such efforts have persisted to present day, but, currently, there is no single text that represents all Buddhist traditions.

Christianity-

The *New Testament* is the newest section of the Christian Bible, the first being the *Old Testament*. The original texts were written by various authors 45 CE in Koine Greek, the written language of the Roman Empire.

The individual books were gradually collected into a single volume. Although Christian denominations differ as to which works are included in the *New Testament*, the majority have settled on the same twenty-seven book canon: it consists of the four narratives of the life and death of Jesus, called "Gospels"; a narrative of the Apostles' ministries in the early church; twenty-one early letters or the "epistles" written by various authors and consisting mostly of Christian counsel and instruction; and an Apocalyptic prophecy.

Hindu-

Hindu scriptures were transmitted orally for many centuries before they were scribed. Sages refined the teachings and expanded the canon. Most sacred texts are in Sanskrit and are classified into two classes: Shruti and Smriti (Vivekananda, 1987).

Shruti (that which is heard) primarily refers to the *Vedas*, which form the earliest record of the Hindu scriptures. They are the laws of the spiritual world, which still exist. Hindus believe that because the spiritual truths of the *Vedas* are eternal, they continue to be expressed in new ways. - There are four *Vedas*: the

Rig-Veda is the first and most important *Veda*. Each *Veda* is divided into four parts: the primary one or the *Veda* proper contains sacred mantras. The other three parts contain commentaries. The *Brahmanas* explain how to perform Vedic rituals. The *Arayakas* and the *Upanishads* are philosophies that discuss the significance of the Vedic rituals. While the *Vedas* focus on rituals, the *Upanishads* focus on spiritual insight and philosophical teachings, and discuss Brahman and reincarnation.

Hindu texts other than the Shrutis are collectively called the Smritis (memory). The most notable of the Smritis are the epics, which consist of the *Mahabharata* and the *Ramayana*, which is the epic story of Prince Rama. The *Bhagavad-Gita* is an integral part of the *Mahabharata* and one of the most popular sacred texts of Hinduism. It contains philosophical teachings from Krishna, an incarnation of Vishnu, told to the prince, Arjuna, on the eve of a great war. The *Bhagavad-Gita*, spoken by Krishna, is described as the essence of the *Vedas*.

Islam-

Muslims consider the *Qur'an* to be the literal word of God; it is the central religious text of Islam. God revealed the verses of the Qur'an to Muhammad through the angel, Gabriel, between 610 and 632 C.E.. Muhammad's companions orally transcribed the *Qur'an* while he was alive. Islamic scholars believe the *Qur'an* has not changed significantly over the years (Esposito 2002).

The *Qur'an* is divided into 114 suras, or chapters, which combined, contain 6,236 verses. The earlier suras, revealed at Mecca, are primarily concerned with ethical and spiritual topics. The later Medinan suras discuss social and moral issues relevant to the Muslim community. The *Qur'an* is more concerned with moral guidance than legal instruction, and is considered the sourcebook of Islamic principles and values.

Judaism-

The Jewish Bible is called the *Tanakh,* which is derived from the three consonants, T, N and K, which represent the Torah, Nevi'im, and Ketuvim, respectively. Torah means law or teaching, and it refers to the whole of the Jewish Bible, which includes the first five books: Genesis, Exodus, Leviticus, Numbers, and Deuteronomy. Nevi'im, or prophets, refers to the twenty-one books, which record the sayings that remind Israel of its relationship with God. Ketuvim, or other writings, refers to the thirteen books that comprise the balance (Novak 1995).

Taoism-

The *Tao Te Ching* is considered to be the most influential Taoist text. It is a foundational scripture of central importance in Taoism. It has been used as a ritual text throughout the history of religious Taoism. The precise date it was written is the subject of debate; thought to be some time between the sixth and third century BCE.

Tao literally means "path" or "way" and can figuratively mean "essential nature," "destiny," "principle," or "true path." The philosophical and religious "Tao" is infinite, without limitation. One view states that the paradoxical opening is intended to prepare the reader for teachings about the unteachable Tao. Tao is believed to be transcendent, indistinct, and without form; therefore, it cannot be named or categorized.

The *Tao Te Ching* is not thematically ordered; however, the main themes of the text are repeated, often with only slight variation. The leading themes revolve around the nature of Tao and how to attain it (Dyer 2007).

Chapter Five

Unifying Principles of the Twelve Steps of A.A. in the Wisdom Traditions

Presented in this section is the research or compendium of discovery which presents the unifying principles, beliefs, and practices explored in eight wisdom traditions as they relate to each of the Twelve Steps of A.A. They are viewed through the lens of each wisdom tradition: Buddhism, Christianity, Cosmology, Hinduism, Islam, Judaism, Native American, and Taoism. The findings are presented, not in an approach that promotes the interpretation of the reader of this document, who is most likely an American-born, Anglo-Saxon, Protestant; but purposefully presented in the contextual language of each wisdom tradition to enhance the understanding of the diverse global population of potential users of the mandala on the website (www.12wisdom-steps.com).

Step 1: We admitted we were powerless over our addiction, that our lives had become unmanageable.
> **Definition**: To truly heal and recover one's well being, one must concede to their innermost self that they are truly powerless.

Honesty—the First Unifying Principle of the Twelve Wisdom Steps

The first principle on which the Twelve Steps were built is honesty because of its foundational quality. Without honesty, our internal house is built on sand. Honesty comes to us from the French word, "honour," which translates as "better." Better than what, we ask? Perhaps, better than what we thought we could ever be; better than we hoped we could become. This implies a couple of spiritual principles inherent in this line of thinking: that we have the capacity for transcendence and that there is an inner knowing reflecting the essence of who we really are. Central to Ken Wilber's work (psychologist, philosopher, and founder of Integral Institute () is the tenet that evolution's path of transcendence is inclusive of all that has gone before it. And this is so true of the path of recovery. Without the learning and realization that come through the honesty of looking at our past behaviors and owning them all, we cannot transcend to the next higher level of our own development.

Truth and trust share the same root derivation – true. When we are not in right alignment with our own truth, we do not trust ourselves to make good decisions and to take the right steps, nor can anyone else trust us to do so. When we become honest and stand in the truth, no matter how messy or difficult, trust is built.

Eastern cultures differentiate truth by defining illusion. The Sufi perspective defines the First Step experience with clarity. They believe by opening our vision to those places that we have attempted to ignore, we are removing the veils of illusion. This can be a heartrending experience, but it also arouses our capacity to feel, which is essential to awakening the love for God that is the core of the Sufi experience.

Buddhism

In the First Noble Truth, the Buddha said life is full of suffering (*dukkha*). Dukkha arises out of ignorance, which leads to thoughts, which lead to consciousness, which generate feelings, that generate desires or cravings, which create grasping or attachment, which create the condition of dukkha. Step One is the process of recognizing this Truth. Buddha said we should respond to this Truth by seeing it clearly, not shying away from the pain, but understanding the cause(s) of our suffering. Buddha recognized that even in our moments of fulfillment, we are grasping toward more (Gerhards 2007).

Christianity

Step One is the admission that we are dependent on God's will. It requires that we unequivocally place our faith in Him. When we are misguided or self-absorbed, we discover we have placed our faith in other people, money, status, power, or notoriety. This step recognizes this misplaced faith has not worked, and in fact, has caused our lives to become unmanageable (Selby 2000).

Cosmology

We admit we are powerless over an addicted society and that our lives and all of life have become degraded. When the consumption of anything is killing us and we cannot stop, we are addicted. We are one with the Earth, and the Earth is becoming toxic. This poisoning is the result of overproduction and over consumption. According to cultural historian, Thomas Berry, the main reason we find ourselves in such ecological chaos is because we are in between stories. "We are out of touch with our true and larger Self." We have not integrated what we are learning about the Cosmos from science into our existing creation story (LaChance 1991).

Hinduism

Human predicament is marked by ignorance (*avidya*), desire, and aversion. How do we, who are Brahman, fail to know what we are? People are ignorant of their true identity as Brahman. We fail to understand our true nature. We are driven by desire for that which promises to fulfill the needs of our body and mind. Without liberating knowledge, human behavior is much like animal behavior – being driven by instinctual desires and aversions (Viswanathan 1992).

Islam

The *Qur'an* frequently depicts unbelievers as having hearts that are diseased. This belief is in alignment with the medical model of addiction – for those who meet the criteria of dependence, it is a disease. It also aligns with the fundamental belief that those who do not have spirituality in their life, experience disease for which they continually seek external means of fulfillment. In Islam, Allah provides the solution, which again parallels the Third Step – submission to the will of Allah (Caner 2002).

Judaism

This step follows in the footsteps of our ancestors. When the Jews were poised at the edges of the Red Sea with the Egyptian armies in pursuit, they panicked. The Israelites were afraid to cross. Moses cajoled them, but to no avail. Fearful that they had come so far only to perish in the waters, our ancestors were ready to return to Egypt and again become enslaved. This may also be our fear. With this step, we stand at the threshold of the Red Sea every day – struggling, fighting the urge to return to the slavery of our dependency (Olitsky 1991).

Native American Spirituality

Because of my dependence on alcohol, I have been unable to care for myself and my family (White Bison 2002).

Taoism

The focus of the twelfth Verse of the *Tao Te Ching* reminds us that allowing the desires of our senses to drive our actions results in excesses and a loss of connection with our inner truth. Because everything in our world is transitory, it is easy to chase appearances and illusions and be distracted from what has meaning and purpose. Dr. Dyer, in *Change your Thoughts, Change your Life*, translates this simply to mean, "We cannot know the creator if we're focused exclusively on what is created." The Tao provides a clear description of the power of addiction, "the chase and the hunt craze people's minds." It goes on to affirm that it is a waste of energy, which in the end impedes our emotional and spiritual development. If we live according to the Tao, we learn to live in the world, but not to be solely of the world because we no longer allow it to be the master of our choices. Our senses become instruments through which we experience the world, broadening and deepening our appreciation and gratitude for its diversity and abundance (Dyer 2007).

Step 2: Came to believe that a Power greater than ourselves could restore us to sanity.
> **Definition**: Hope is the first step in discovering the solution, which is identifying with a power that can help dispel the obsession created by the addiction. The gift in this step is discovering and believing that change is possible.

Hope—the Second Unifying Principle of the Twelve Wisdom Steps

The universal principle of the Second Step is Hope. Before we can actually grasp hope, we must first recognize that the situation we are in is untenable. We must have a firm conviction that there is a cause to our suffering and that change is possible; a belief that we can create a different experience. At this point, we may or may not recognize how much internal fortitude it might take, that most of the change will be accomplished by us – not the conditions outside ourselves. This ambiguity may in fact be beneficial by not impeding our motivation to take the first steps needed to initiate the change process.

Many words pregnant with spiritual meaning define Hope: expectation, trust, reliance, promise, confidence, possibility, and desire. From England and Scotland, we learn the word has geographic significance: describing a bay or inlet, and a plateau between mountains. These derivations paint a visual picture of a haven safe from the storm, a resting place, a promised land of quietude reached after trekking the rigors of the mountain passes.

Hope is a complex principle that requires recognizing there is a life-impacting or threatening problem, desiring a different outcome, holding the vision of what is possible, and stepping into the solution or change process with desire and expectation.

And lastly, this principle asks us to trust that there is a power that will sustain and support us. As we study the interpretations of the Second Step in the wisdom traditions, we see there are many affirmations assuring us that we are not alone.

In Christianity, it is the realization that Christ is ready and available at any time to be in relationship with us. In Cosmology, we trust the evolutionary process of the Originating Mystery. In Hinduism, we learn that Brahman will liberate us from *samsara*, the karmic cycle. In Islam, Allah guides one's spiritual path to liberation and salvation. In the remaining traditions that are ethics based, Buddhism, Judaism, Native American, and Taoism, the focus leans more towards our gaining an awareness that change is possible, acquiring knowledge, and making the right choices and decisions.

Once again, we are reminded by the wisdom underlying the Twelve Steps that each step is an action step, calling us to be proactive in our own transformation.

Buddhism

In the Second Noble Truth, the Buddha tells us the cause of our suffering is our ceaseless desire for pleasure (*tanha*) and ignorance (*avijja*). The abandonment of desire is a core value of Buddhist practice. For suffering to end, we must learn how to cease our craving, and acquire the wisdom we do not have. Suffering is caused by our desire to have things be different than they are; it is a grasping for self-satisfaction and fulfillment from external sources (Gerhards 2007).

Christianity

Step Two is focused on developing a personal relationship with Jesus Christ. It is a relationship that transcends rational understanding and belief. It is an experiential realization that Christ cares for and about us and is ready and available at any time to be in relationship with us. This relationship encompasses love, forgiveness, comfort, guidance, and direction (Selby 2000).

Cosmology

It is time for us to integrate what we are learning from science about the Cosmos into our existing creation story. Thomas Berry, cultural historian, observed, "For peoples generally, their story of the universe and the human role within the universe is their primary source of intelligibility and value. Only through this story of how the universe came to be in the beginning, and how it came to be as it is, does a person come to appreciate the meaning of life or to derive the psychic energy needed to deal effectively with those crisis moments that occur in the life of the individual and in the life of the society (Berry 2000).

Hinduism

Atman is the eternal light of consciousness that illumines the mind. It is not the mind; this Atman is Brahman. The goal of spiritual discipline is knowledge (*jnana*) of the identity between one's true Self (the higher Self) and Brahman, which leads to liberation from (*samsara*) the cycle of birth and death perpetuated by karma. The true Self is the light of consciousness that shines deep within the mind. The true Self is changeless. The journey home is impossible without external assistance because the conditions of captivity are so disorienting that the deluded are unable to find their way home under their own power (Viswanathan 1992).

Islam

Muslims wholeheartedly believe that Allah will show them the path to liberation and salvation. "God guides to the right path whomever He wants," (2:213). However, it requires that each person make his or her spiritual path and work a lifetime work. The results are not up to God, but a combination of God's mercy and man's right actions. "Those who seek the protection of God will certainly be guided to the right path," (3:101). The path is described by Allah as an "uphill path" and outlines the required works: freeing people in bondage, helping those in need, and feeding the poor (Dawood 1956).

Judaism

Jews have always known that belief is essential, but that doesn't mean it's easy. Our tradition tells us the one power God withholds, even from Godself, is the power to make us believe. Difficulty in faith is not failure. Look at the story of the golden calf where we turned our backs on God after God brought us out of Egypt. How far is it from creating and idolizing the golden drug or bottle to the original golden calf? Perhaps there is no difference. The sages pointed out that there are many kinds and forms of golden calves in our lives (Olitsky 1991).

Native American Spirituality

There is hope no matter how much misery and despair we feel. God can help, but we must do our part. The Creator has gifted us with free will, and the power of choice, which must be in alignment with our goals (White Bison 2002).

Taoism

"Knowing ignorance is strength. Ignoring knowledge is sickness." The seventy-first verse of the Tao touches the heart of the paradox of addiction and recovery in the words "only when we are sick of our sickness shall we cease to be sick." It is only when we become fully aware that we are sick in mind, body, and spirit that we can cease to be sick, because only when we are equipped with this knowledge are we ready to consider changing the fundamental cause. Knowledge provides us strength; ignorance of the truth perpetuates our dis-ease. When we experience dis-ease in mind, body, or spirit, it is because some aspect of our life is out of balance. The next step is to identify where we are living in excess and what is being ignored as a consequence (Mitchell 1988).

Step 3: Made a decision to turn our will and our lives over to the care of God as we understood Him.

Definition: Faith requires making a decision that will solve the problem.

Faith—the Third Unifying Principle of the Twelve Wisdom Steps

Faith is fundamental to all traditions. It requires belief or trust and often requires trust before belief can materialize. A universal understanding across traditions is a belief in a transcendent or supreme being. This belief is often viewed as unfounded because there is not always logical proof or material evidence. Cosmology requires us to trust what science can prove, but which is not observable to the naked eye – a subatomic unifying oneness, a universal energy that is the rudimentary matter of all that exists.

As we seek interpretation and meaning from the Wisdom traditions, we discover several common themes. The first is surrender or the giving up or letting go of one's will or need to control. Taoism helps us realize that our need for control comes from fear; the fear of our own inability to handle what we are not ready or prepared for. When we are rigid in our need to control, we often encounter resistance and disappointment. There is a natural rhythm and flow of life, and when we align ourselves with it, we are able to let go of stress, worry, and fear. We begin to rely on a power greater than ourselves.

The Three Noble Truths in Buddhism provide a practical application of this step. The 3rd Truth helps us understand that when we let go of craving and attachment to what we want and desire, our pain will dissolve. And gaining an awareness that impermanence or change is actually the constant in life provides hope and the ability to trust that change is possible. This is the Third Step.

The first three words of this step are the most critical to its application and practice: "Made a decision." Faith requires commitment, and commitment often waivers. We have doubts, we falter, stop, restart, and begin again. Faith is a journey that takes us from a place of denial, resistance, struggle, and doubt to one of testing, acceptance, commitment, and surrender. Christianity names the process "repentance" which means to "rethink" (*penser*) or to learn a new way of thinking or a new perspective.

Hinduism helps us understand that our unique identity is not superior; that we in fact are one with Spirit (Brahman) and when we can subjugate our infatuation with self, we become open to the light of consciousness, which will illumine the mind and reveal our Higher Self.

We benefit from the practice of worship in all religions/traditions because we are reminded that we are not gods and there is a Higher Being. Our humility increases and we are open and available to be in relationship with this Being.

Buddhism

In the Third Noble Truth, the Buddha tells us desire ends when we let go of craving and attachment; the pain will dissolve. When we gain a deep understanding that all things in life are impermanent, unsatisfying and without eternal substance, we are ready to start letting go of our attachment to the conditions and our desire for change. We cannot experience Nirvana or bliss until we let go of our clinging nature (Gerhards 2007).

Christianity

Step Three is an action step. Many analogies used to explain the Twelve Steps describe Step One as the diagnosis, Step Two as the prescription, and Step Three as following the various steps prescribed by the physician in order to heal. This step requires a submission of one's will to follow directions and guidance from a source outside oneself. When we apply this analogy to our larger life, it means we surrender our need to control every last detail and allow ourselves to be guided by Divine will. In Christianity, this surrender is often called repentance. Repentance comes from the Latin word *penser* or ponder, meaning "to re-think." It requires us to rethink who is actually in charge of our lives, our destiny, our eternity (Selby 2000).

Cosmology

In an evolving universe everything is constantly in a state of flux; nothing is static, nothing remains the same. Science demonstrates this at a subatomic level; everything is vibrational energy; however, our eyes and our minds trick us into believing it is constant because matter appears dense and static. This is precisely why we need faith. We need to trust in the unseen, the Mystery (Dowd 2008).

Hinduism

Liberation (*moksa*) comes from living a life of right action by following the guidance of the scriptures. The Veda is considered to be the only source of valid knowledge. Liberation means liberation from one's body (*sariratva*). The individual soul must rely on the Lord, who is the ultimate cause of all action. It requires one to surrender their conventional identity and to identify oneself wholly with Brahman. Liberation is another word for Brahman. Knowledge of Brahman is the removal of ignorance. Liberating knowledge is the insight that one truly is Brahman. Scripture teaches that Brahman is the light of consciousness that illumines the mind and, therefore, is the true Self; that knowledge is the cure for the disease of suffering caused by ignorance (Viswanathan 1992).

Islam

Faith in Islam is called *Iman*. It requires complete submission to the will of God (Allah), which includes belief, profession, and full commitment to Allah's will. Iman has two aspects: recognizing and affirming that there is only one Creator of the universe and worshipping only this Creator. According to Islamic thought, this comes naturally because faith is an instinct of the human soul. The other aspect is willingness and a commitment to Allah and His prescriptions for living (Caner 2002).

Judaism

Some people think faith in God comes easily. For Jews, belief in God is a struggle. We spend our lives trying to figure out the range and shape of that belief, what it means, and how it compels us to act. We start by making a decision to believe. You will have doubts; we all do. Throughout the Jewish calendar year, we are given opportunities to start again, to make *teshuvah*, a turning toward God. Before *Rosh Hashanah* and Yom Kippur, we get ready to shed our past and begin our journey toward personal repair. Scripture captures this time when fearfulness can be transformed: "When God began to create…the world was chaotic, without order. And so, God drew near to the chaos and brought light to the world in order to illumine the darkness," (Olitsky 1991).

Native American Spirituality

This Step focuses on seeking help and guidance from an elder, a medicine person, a sponsor, a mentor, or a spiritual friend. Allow your eyes, ears, and heart to guide you to the right person who can understand and support you (White Bison 2002).

Taoism

In the Taoist way, we come to understand that when we force an outcome, we are going against the flow of life, and in doing so, we often encounter resistance, disappointment, and, often, suffering. It often feels like we are pushing to no avail. When we surrender, we are letting go of the need to control everybody and everything around us. The need for control comes from fear; the fear of our own inability to handle what we are not ready or prepared for. There is a natural rhythm in the flow of life, and when we find it, we are able to effortlessly keep in step. Only then do we live our lives by letting go of stress, worries, and fears, trusting in a power greater than ourselves (Dyer 2007).

Step 4: Made a searching and fearless moral inventory of our selves.

> **Definition:** Courage is the ability to confront fear, pain, danger, uncertainty, or intimidation. Moral courage is the ability to act with integrity in the face of shame, scandal, or discouragement.

Courage—the Fourth Unifying Principle of the Twelve Wisdom Steps

Courage derives from the Latin and French word "heart." The heart is being defined as the seat of intelligence or feelings. And, in order to practice the Fourth step, one is required to have moral courage, which is the ability to act with integrity. In recent years, we have learned much about emotional intelligence and, in fact, when we are in touch with our emotions, we discover they can inform us greatly. Not only do they provide us valuable information about ourselves, they often motivate us to action. Guilt is an emotion inherently connected to the Fourth step and it is seen as a helpful emotion because it motivates us to make right where we have wronged. The Fourth step systemizes the process. It requires that we perform a thorough self-examination and take an "inventory." Both Christianity and Judaism have "confessional" practices, which provide methods with which to take this step.

Every tradition provides tools and guidance that support taking this step. The Eightfold path in Buddhism provides a simple list of Right actions: view, intention, speech, action, livelihood, effort, mindfulness, and concentration. Each of these is further defined by specific practices. For example, Right speech requires abstaining from lying, slander, abusive and harsh speech, and idle chatter or gossip. The Ten Commandments provide the basic values and actions for living a Christian life.

Hinduism helps us shift our focus from our corporal self and its needs and wants to a higher consciousness through meditation practices. This tradition clearly states that ignorance of our true (spiritual) nature is the cause of our suffering and we will remain in bondage until we are enlightened through spiritual practices.

The *Qur'an*, the holy book of Islam, is primarily a book of rules, laws, and requirements of how to live one's life. The Five Pillars of Islam include specific daily requirements of praise and prayer. Muslims, first and foremost, are required to be obedient to the Laws of Islam.

And, fundamental to all traditions, is the aspiration of living one's life in integrity, which means one's actions are in alignment with one's values. And, our living values should be integral with our spiritual values.

Buddhism

The Precepts, the Hindrances, and the Eightfold Path are all available for taking inventory. Classic Buddhist inventory uses the training precepts. These are the fundamental moral principles the Buddha taught to avoid creating negative karma. This step requires making a decision to follow the Buddhist path of liberation by taking refuge in the practice of wakefulness, truth, and fellowship (Gerhards 2007).

Christianity

It takes courage to look at the truth about ourselves – our character defects and our strengths. The process of sanctification (being healed or becoming holy) requires a willingness to know the truth about ourselves. It requires a fearless and thorough self-examination. We need to face the hard questions: Where do we fall short, what is it we are to become, how must we change? What are the attitudes and behaviors that need to be changed? Our ability to rationalize our behavior creates a veil of self-deception. This step pierces this veil, which is often painful but necessary. This step is the fulfillment of the adage, "The truth will set you free," (Selby 2000).

Cosmology

This step asks us to examine our part in how we have harmed the Earth itself and the species with which we share the planet. We must ask ourselves when we have demanded more satisfaction than was our fair and equitable share of the supply (food, water, sex, oil, energy, money, etc.) Only when we take this step personally can we identify our own addictive behaviors and their consequences (LaChance 1991).

Hinduism

Ayida, which is spiritual ignorance of our true nature, is the root cause of our suffering. When we are in bondage to ayida, we experience aversion (*dvesha*), attachment (*raga*), self-centeredness (*asmita*) and fear of death (*abhinivesha*) because we are clinging to life and mistakenly believe our physical bodies are our sole identities. Meditation practice allows our consciousness to expand until we move from the limitations of the self to a wider experience of reality (Viswanathan 1992).

Islam

Righteousness, as taught in the Qur'an, is a commitment to acting in accordance with the will of Allah. Specifically, it means living one's life from a deep sense of justice, equality, and fairness. It encompasses a generosity of spirit and deeds, reaching out to those in need, maintaining one's inner strength to stand firm against the powers of evil, and carefully fulfilling one's duty each day. It is obedience to the Law of Islam (Caner 2002).

Judaism

Taking inventory or confession is called a *cheshbon banefesh*, which is literally an accounting of the soul. Self-examination is an important part of the Jewish tradition. In *Avot de Rabbi Natan*, it is written: "The eye is shown only what it is capable of seeing and the ear hears only what it is capable of listening to," (Olitsky 1991).

Native American Spirituality

Self-examination has always been part of Native culture because the cultural definition of success is centered on building character. Before we can build character, we must know our shortcomings, weaknesses, and character defects. Self-examination takes a warrior's courage. To have courage means to have heart. This step is about finding your heart (White Bison 2002).

Taoism

The thirty-third verse of the Tao asks us to discover who we really are and how we affect others. What is the quality of our relationships with family, friends, community, and Earth? How are our actions impacting others? Are our actions congruent with our values and beliefs or are we acting out of alignment with our inner core belief system? Do we spend more time apprising others than we do evaluating and scrutinizing ourselves? (Mitchell 1988).

Step 5: Admitted to God, to our selves, and to another human being the exact nature of our wrongs.

Definition: Integrity is the quality of having a sense of honesty and truthfulness regarding one's motivations and actions.

Integrity—the Fifth Unifying Principle of the Twelve Wisdom Steps

Integrity is the quality of having a sense of honesty and truthfulness regarding one's motivations and actions. The word is derived from the Latin *integritas*, which means "the state or quality of being complete, unbroken, or whole." The definition also includes moral soundness or honesty, as well as freedom from corruption. It is no wonder that the founders of A.A. made this principle the Fifth step.

Once one musters the courage to perform a self-examination and thorough inventory, it is critical to not only focus on our defects and wrongs, but to also assess our strengths and values. The word "integer" is derived from the same root and means "oneness" or wholeness. When we see ourselves as whole and complete, we must acknowledge that our inner psyche reflects the goodness of our creator. Only when we are able to gain this understanding are we able to see ourselves as whole and complete.

Step Five is the "confessional" step in that it requires verbalizing or sharing the inventory, which was compiled in the Fourth Step. This step is actually based on sound behavioral research. For confession to actually purge or wash away the residual guilt and shame we carry from the harms we have caused, it must have a public element. It must be spoken out loud and heard by another. Only when it is an overt act does the individual experience a lightening of soul and Spirit. Cosmology describes this step as an "emptying" of our selves. Zen Buddhism calls this process *sunyata*. In spiritual terms, it is creating a void or an empty container, which can then be filled with goodness, joy, peace, and Spirit. We know this is true because the field of physics has proven that a void never remains static.

The Muslims perform this step literally with an ablution or cleansing ritual. Preceding prayer, they wash themselves with the *wudu'* ritual, which prepares them for communication with Allah.

In Judaism, we learn that if we do not take these confessional or purging steps, our hearts will harden. When this happens, the heart becomes impermeable; as a result, we can feel nothing. We lose touch with ourselves, and then in turn, we become unreachable by others.

Buddhism

This Step relates to Right speech, which is based on saying only what is true and what is useful. Words are inherently powerful; they have the potential to create and to heal, as well as to harm and destroy (Gerhards 2007).

Christianity

Confession is a critical step in our healing process. It represents the releasing or turning over of that which we no longer want to be; or to carry in our hearts and souls. It is the open, verbal expression of the insights gained from our self-examination to the God of our understanding and one other person. The most difficult aspect of this step is the requirement to share with another human being. Our pride often tells us this is unnecessary, but, in fact, it is critical. It humbles us, and from this experience, we grow stronger in our own integrity. Once we have released our fears, harms, and resentments, we experience a sense of lightness and acceptance. The forgiveness we experience is the gift of grace (Monahan 2001).

Cosmology

Step Five is a "confessional" step designed for us to empty ourselves – to empty our psychic trash. In Zen, this process is called *sunyata*. In spiritual concepts, it is creating a void through emptying. We know from physics that a void is never static; instead, it is always available to be filled. Once we remove the psychic toxins we have been holding, we are ready for the Originating Mystery to recreate us (LaChance 1991).

Hinduism

Dharma is fulfilling one's life purpose. It means doing what you are called to do; doing it ethically, purposefully, and to the best of your ability. In the *Bhagavad-Gita*, Lord Krishna urged Arjuna to pick up his bow and go to war. He was born into a family of kings and warriors, and his brother's kingdom was taken over by a tyrant. This was his dharma (Satchidananda 1988).

Islam

Ablution or cleansing is a ritual (*rak'at*) preceding prayer which Muslims perform in order to purify and ready themselves for prayer. These preparations, known as *wudu'*, are obligatory if water is available. The first step is an acknowledgement of one's obedience to the practice and to Allah. In addition to the washing ritual, one's clothes must be clean, and one must be modestly attired. Allah only hears prayers if one is physically clean (Caner 2002).

Judaism

The Baal Shem Tov has taught us that, through the power of prayer, even the least among us can communicate with God. Every outpouring of the heart, when spoken in earnest and with devotion, is a true prayer. According to the rabbis, one of the effects of transgressions is a hardening of the heart. The heart becomes like a rock, solid and impermeable, feeling nothing. When you begin to admit your wrongs to God, openings develop, like small cracks in a rock. Once our heart begins to open, these cracks begin to widen. Finally, our hearts break open, and the head begins to know what before only the heartfelt (Olitsky 1991).

Native American Spirituality

This step is about disclosing our secrets. When we reveal our secrets to another human being and to the Creator, the heaviness is lifted, and we begin to see with our hearts, just as the eagle sees love in everything. This step deepens our relationship with the Great Spirit (White Bison 2002).

Taoism

The Tao asks us to live beyond our judgment of others. We are given a formula for learning to live harmoniously with each other. It requires us to replace criticism, judgment, and prejudice with acceptance, kindness, and appreciation. This conversion does not happen instantly; it requires practice and discipline. We can begin by replacing our critical and judgmental thoughts with just noticing others without evaluating or assessing them. The next step is to identify something in the other that is similar to yourself. Look for the common ground – focus on the similarities, not the differences. The way of the Tao is to see ourselves in others and to experience the oneness of all creation (Dyer 2007).

Step 6: Were entirely ready to have God remove all these defects of character.
>   **Definition**: Inclined or favorably disposed; ready to act; voluntary; self-determined; intentional.

Willingness—the Sixth Unifying Principle of the Twelve Wisdom Steps

Willingness is described as being inclined or favorably disposed; ready to act; self-determined; or voluntarily intentioned. Superficially, it sounds like we are ready to have a Higher Being remove our defects. And, it would be easy to ask – why not? Sounds easy. You identify your defects, share what they are with someone else, and then ask for them to be washed away. But, in actuality, is it that easy? How attached are we to our "character defects," which are part of our identity; part of our personality and how we present ourselves in the world? Perhaps, one of our defects is pride, and we are proud of who we are and our accomplishments – yes, maybe we have tramped on some toes to get where we are, but look at the status we have achieved. Are we really ready to ask for this aspect of our character to disappear, to go away? Who are we then? Who will we become?

At this point, we may need to go back and revisit the Third Step. Who is in control of our lives? And perhaps we need another look at the First Step – what sources our power? Are we open and willing to transform into something beyond who we are today? The conversion these steps perform, along with other wisdom traditions, is a shift from self-centeredness to being other centered. It requires nothing less than the willingness to work on those character traits that stand in the way of this process.

Buddhism takes this step apart and divides it into a three-fold process: the primary one being detachment from our desires, expectations, and coveted outcomes. It requires having the Right intention, along with renunciation or detachment. This is where the hard work begins. We need to become willing to transform into a persona who is greater than the person we have been.

Buddhism

This Step relates to Right intention, which is a threefold process: the intention of renunciation or detachment; the intention of good will; and the intention of harmlessness. These three are opposed to three parallel kinds of wrong intention: intention led by desire, by ill will, and by harmfulness. Just prior to the Buddha's enlightenment, he reflected that his thoughts could be separated into these two distinct groups (right and wrong). When those of the second kind arose, he saw that they brought distress to himself or to others – or to both. They obstructed wisdom and led away from freedom. But whenever those of the first kind arose, they were clearly beneficial, conducive to the growth of wisdom and an aid to the attainment of Nirvana (Gerhards 2007).

Christianity

This step reminds us that we always have a choice – we were given free will. We can take the softer, easier way and do what we have always done with the same results, or we can make the hard decision to do what is right. This is the human struggle. This step requires us to live and grow in the integrity and values of our faith. It requires conviction. The previous steps have, however, prepared us through the practices of repentance, self-examination, and confession. We have also come to believe that we are not powerless, knowing that God is an indwelling presence that provides us with a well of strength and hope (Selby 2000).

Cosmology

We become entirely willing to have all habits of illusion removed from our thoughts, attitudes, and behaviors. We become willing to allow the Originating Mystery to transform us from within, from being self-centered to other-centered (LaChance 1991).

Hinduism

There are several ways of making amends for misdeeds from one's past: meditation that releases karmic energy from the body; contemplating the divine qualities of a favorite deity; and chanting the sounds resonant with divinity to purify one's consciousness and neutralize it from negative karmas. This practice is considered sacrificial because it requires taking our time to focus on God and divine qualities, self-reflection, and surrender to the Divine Will with gratitude and humility (Viswanathan 1992).

Islam

Fasting is performed by Muslims in obedience to Allah. It helps Muslims learn the practices of discipline and self-restraint. It also clears the mind and the body and readies it for open and receptive communication with Allah through prayer and meditation (Caner 2002).

Judaism

Our character defects define us and protect us at the same time. Thus, we fear their loss would leave us fragmented, empty, and vulnerable. When the early descendants of Adam corrupted the world, God saw fit to wash it clean. We rely on God to send for spiritual waters to cleanse us, to wash away our transgressions. Each time we see a rainbow, we are reminded of God's promise always to help cleanse us. God spanned the rainbow across the heavens to serve as an eternal reminder of His connection with us. We recite continually in our hearts: *Baruch ata Adonai, zocher ha-brit* (Praised are You, Adonai, upon whom we rely to remember this covenant.) (Olitsky 1991).

Native American Spirituality

This step consolidates the process of self-discovery through which we identified our character defects and weaknesses. Now we are entirely ready to release them (White Bison 2002).

Taoism

The heart of this step reminds us that all we need to do to change is take the first step. It is often the hardest step, but once it is taken, those that follow become easier. It also reminds us that we can't go back and do-over what is already done. All we ever have is now, this moment. This practice is also at the heart of the Twelve Steps, which emphasizes living one day at a time, and concentrating only on doing the next right thing. One step, one moment, one day at a time is the way of the Tao (Dyer 2007).

Step 7: Humbly asked Him to remove our shortcomings.

Definition: Freedom from pride and arrogance; lowliness of mind; a modest estimate of one's own self-worth; an act of submission.

Humility—the Seventh Unifying Principle of the Twelve Wisdom Steps

Humility and humus, meaning ground, soil or earth, share the same root derivation. We turn to Islam to help us understand humility in its spiritual context. The word "Islam" means "surrender," which is at the heart of this tradition – surrender to Allah. Muslims are called to prayer five times daily. They bow prostrate facing Mecca and chant the *Dhikr*, a long invocation of the names of God. The reason for bowing and prostrating is to surrender the ego – to lower it to the plane of the Earth (the ground), which is an externalized act acknowledging the supremacy of Allah and the resultant humility or humbleness of humans in his Presence. It is the ultimate act of submission in this life, which prepares us for the final one. Cosmology reminds us that we are earth; we plant, harvest, and eat the products of the Earth and when we die, we compost into soil again.

In Native American spirituality, humility is defined as an attitude required in making a fresh start. It helps us face life with a beginner's mind, which is also a characteristic valued in Buddhism. Buddhism and Taoism emphasize the value of having balance in one's life and being balanced in our lifestyle. The law of karma reveals that when there is an excessive force, it will be counterbalanced by its opposite. Hence, a prideful ego sets us up for a fall, which prevents us and others from benefiting from our appreciation and gratitude.

When we live humbly, we avoid excesses, knowing how much is enough. We know when to stop and when to let go. We develop mindfulness and are able to find joy in any moment.

Buddhism

This Step relates to Right view. Right view develops in stages. We commonly begin our quest for truth through a direct insight into the first Truth – suffering. Our habitual views are challenged and appear lacking. Our search begins. We come to appreciate that some of our views are wrong, and we modify our actions (karma) accordingly. More wholesome actions bring stability of mind, which inclines us toward reflection and meditation, which in turn deepens our understanding. The process is a gradual one. It requires understanding the Five Aggregates and learning self-management of them: body, feelings, perceptions, mental formations, and consciousness (Gerhards 2007).

Christianity

At first, change is difficult; this is true for everyone. The First Step in the change process is willingness to change. This step is based on humility, because at the core of this practice, is the realization that we can't do it alone. We need the support of others who understand, we need a path of practices like the Twelve Steps or the 10 Commandments, and we need to know that the strength we require comes from the indwelling Presence of God. Our personal transformation will only happen if we learn to ask for help: from others and from God through the words and intentions of our prayers. Through prayer, we ask for our needs, for the Highest and best good for all concerned, and we express gratitude for these and all the gifts we have received from His bounty and grace (Monahan 2001).

Cosmology

This step calls for us to be humble. Humility comes from the word humus or soil. Humility helps us recognize that we come from the soil. We are earthness. We plant, harvest, and eat the products of the soil. When we die, we compost into soil again (Dowd 2008).

Hinduism

People need to hear revealed truth and be taught the meaning of the truth by a guru(s) so they can gain understanding and reach enlightenment. A compassionate wise teacher must remove the blindfolds of delusion that keep a person imprisoned in the forest of the body (Viswanathan 1992).

Islam

The body of Islamic law as a whole is known as Shari'a, which means path. According to Islam this is a divinely appointed path explicitly laid out for humanity to follow in order to reach salvation. It has two primary sources, the *Qur'an* and the *Sunna*. The *Sunna* is significant to the spirituality of Islam because it teaches Muslims how Muhammad acted during his life. The *Sunna* addresses ways of life dealing with friends, family, and government (Dawood 1956).

Judaism

Humility is one of Judaism's precepts. How can we not be humbled by God's awesome presence? Jews cover their heads to constantly remind themselves there is a greater Power. We bow the head and bend the knee in prayer to remind ourselves that we are not in control, God is. To be humble is to speak from the strength of one's limitations (Olitsky 1991).

Native American Spirituality

At this point in the warrior's journey, we have the knowledge, desire, and allies to change. The self-knowledge comes from the inventories and lists made while facing south. Our allies are the sobriety elders and the Red Road brothers and sisters we've been sitting with in sobriety and healing circles. And, now, we are also walking each day with our Creator. Humility is an attitude that will help us start fresh in everything we do. It helps us face life with a beginner's or learner's mind. One of the tools to help us is writing and repeating affirmations (White Bison 2002).

Taoism

The verses of the *Tao Te Ching* help us view our lives through the filter of balance, which is a fundamental principle of the Tao. It helps us understand when enough is sufficient and that within the natural order there is enough. Excess upsets the balance. Our own excesses upset the balance in our lives. A prideful ego sets us up for a fall, which is the natural consequence of this excessive behavior when it pushes out the appreciation and acclamation of others and their efforts and contributions. If we live our lives humbly, we know how much is enough, when to stop, and when to let go. In living our lives mindfully, we can find joy in any moment (Dyer 2007).

Step 8: Made a list of all persons we had harmed, and became willing to make amends to them all.

> **Definition:** Personal attachment; that which commands admiration; sympathetic understanding; ardent affection; the earnest effort to promote the welfare of others.

Love—the Eighth Unifying Principle of the Twelve Wisdom Steps

There are two definitions of love, which address the spirit of this step:

1. sympathetic understanding, and
2. earnest effort to promote the welfare of others.

Love is the underlying principle of this step because it is fundamental to the process of listing all the persons we have harmed and gaining determination to make amends. The first requirement is to have nurtured enough self-love to begin this step (which is the natural outcome of having completed the previous seven steps) and to trust in the love expressed as sympathy and understanding that others have towards those who are truly willing to own their wrongs and make them right.

Tonglen is a contemplative Tibetan practice of compassion, which asks us to imagine we are in another's shoes, in order to better understand their experience. This is a recommended practice for anyone beginning this step. It is easy for our rational minds to minimize the impact we have had on others; and to fully engage in this step, it is paramount that we own the consequences to fully make reparation in kind.

Many believe that an apology suffices, but what we learn from the wisdom traditions is that matching restitution or reparation is required, and it is preferable to do this face-to-face, looking the other in the eye.

Some people are concerned about the inequality and injustices rampant in our world. It is easy to become complacent and ineffectual because the problem appears too large to influence. This step reminds us that we can address injustices in our own lives in a very tangible way, and like many larger problems, we can "begin to be the change we want to see" in the world.

Taoism provides us the symbol of the yin and yang in which we find a speck of light in the darkness. This symbol visually demonstrates that what we need in order to change (courage, honesty, wisdom, humility) is always found within. When we follow the way of the Tao, we are able to let go of anger and resentment and create space for love and kindness to flow.

Buddhism

An awakened person maintains a heart filled with loving kindness toward all beings. One does not view anyone as an "enemy." All beings are seen through the eyes of compassion and are treated with kindness. The Dalai Lama is the ultimate modern day example of one who not only embodies love and compassion, but demonstrates how to extend it to those who hate and deem to destroy the Tibetan people and their religious beliefs. He says repeatedly, "My religion is love" (Rahula 1959).

Christianity

Making amends or making restitution is an action step. Many think an apology might suffice. Amends, much like Step Five (confession), is a humbling step through which we must own and be accountable for the effects or consequences of our behaviors on others and make every effort to right the wrong. If we have stolen monies or property, then we must replace what we have taken plus add one-fifth to it (much like we pay interest on debt). The result of having performed this step is freedom from guilt and shame, which would otherwise remain alive and buried in our emotional psyche (Selby 2000).

Cosmology

We trust that the Originating Mystery inherent in all matter causes life to self-organize, self-evolve, and self-regulate. We humans need to allow this process to evolve (LaChance 1991).

Hinduism

Seeing divinity in everything means having a vision of equality. There are no judgments, no rankings, no categorizing, no labeling, no duality. The sage sees everyone as he sees Self. It becomes easier to "Love your neighbor as your Self." This practice requires that we actually see ourselves in others – in order to find the common ground of our being-ness. It also requires that we know and love ourselves, without which we cannot know or love another. A God-realized person sees nothing but God everywhere because there is only one Universal truth grounded in love (Viswanathan 1992).

Islam

Muslims practice gratitude for Creation and all that it encompasses. They show their humility for what they have received. Their prayers reflect their gratitude for all they have been given from daily guidance to the creation of the universe. Believers follow the example of Prophet Solomon who prayed with deep gratitude, saying "Lord, inspire me to thank you for your favors to me and my parents and to act righteously so as to please You," (Caner 2002).

Judaism

Lists imply order. Some people think there is too much order in Judaism. But Jews believe that if we follow a specific way of doing things, an order that has worked for so many for so long, we have a better chance of reaching our goals. We are taught that part of our task is to restore order and goodness to the world. We have a powerful compulsion to mend the world's imperfections. This step prepares us to begin making the world a better place by correcting the injustice that has come from what we have or haven't done through our own actions (Olitsky 1991).

Native American Spirituality

This step helps us start to mend the wreckage of our relationships. We acknowledge that we have hurt people. We prepare the ground to actually make amends in the next step. We understand we are connected to all things. When we accept this truth, we become willing to look at our part in the creation of the harm. Each person who wronged us or we wronged is carefully considered, respected, and honored. To honor one is to honor all, and to dishonor one is to dishonor all (White Bison 2002).

Taoism

When there is hurt, "someone must risk returning injury with kindness, or hostility will never turn to goodwill." There must be an offering of kindness, love, and authentic forgiveness. The cosmos continuously demonstrates that within chaos, we find tranquility and vice-versa. This is characterized in the symbol of the yin and yang. Within the darkness, we find a speck of light. As we come to live in the way of the Tao, we learn to let go of anger and resentment in order to create space for love and kindness to flow. Source is always giving, always creating, and new life is always emerging. This is the way of the universe (Dyer 2007).

Step 9: Made direct amends to such people wherever possible, except when to do so would injure them or others.

Definition: the quality of dealing justly between people; integrity; perfect social harmony; the practice of virtue toward others; equitableness; fairness; impartiality

Justice—the Ninth Unifying Principle of the Twelve Wisdom Steps

Justice is the principle of equity, fairness, and impartiality. The practice of the Ninth step is actually affecting justice. It is the act of reparation – repairing or restoring; giving satisfaction or providing compensation for a wrong or injury. Restitution is the restoring of anything to its rightful owner or providing an equivalent for any loss.

We turn to the wisdom of the Native Americans for a practical "how to" guide in making our amends.

- Talk to an elder (sponsor, mentor) for advice on what would constitute reparation of equal value
- Also seek another's opinion to ensure that by making amends, you are not creating more hurt or harm
- Rehearse what you are going to say
- When making amends, keep to your script; be short, direct, and to the point
- If someone has passed, amends can be done through prayer and sometimes restitution can be paid forward to another (relative, organization, etc.)

The practice in Judaism contributes a few additional steps, which you may want to incorporate:

- Be ready to listen to how hurt and angry they were
- Ask what you can do to make things right
- Remember you are not responsible for the outcome; approach the   exchange without expectations
- If further hurt or harm is a consideration, there are times it is appropriate to make amends anonymously

Judaism emphasizes that our deeds are far more important than our thoughts or words. They believe who we are is equal to what we do. Making amends heals the world and us. It allows us to restore shalom (peace), unity, and wholeness.

Buddhism

Remorse is one of the Five Hindrances, which are obstacles to meditation, happiness, and our ability to lead satisfying lives. During meditation, we come to understand their power and begin to develop skills to overcome them so they no longer have power over our thoughts and actions (Gerhards 2007).

Christianity

Making amends or making restitution is an action step. Many think an apology might suffice. Amends, much like Step five (confession), is a humbling step through which we must own and be accountable for the effects or consequences of our behaviors on others and make every effort to right the wrong. If we have stolen monies or property, then we must replace what we have taken plus add one-fifth to it (much like we pay interest on debt). The result of having performed this step is freedom from guilt and shame, which would otherwise remain alive and buried in our emotional psyche (Selby 2000).

Cosmology

We move into action. We become an active part of the healing of the planet. Many will discover the giving of ourselves was what we longed for all our lives. We become filled with the marvelous power of hope. We join others in the great work of renewing the Earth and we begin to experience community again (Berry 2000).

Hinduism

All human beings have five debts we need to repay during our lifetimes. We must express our gratitude to the gods for their blessings by honoring them through ritual. We must pay the debt we owe our parents and teachers by supporting them, and passing on their knowledge to our children. We treat guests visiting our homes as if they are deities. We treat all human beings with respect, which is their due. We offer help to those who are in need (Viswanathan 1992).

Islam

Almsgiving (*zakat*) is also a form of purification that cleanses the Muslim of greed and selfishness, while requiring an equitable sharing of goods with the entire community. The purpose is to create unity and an understanding of the community as one interdependent whole. Zakat is critical to one's salvation. If a Muslim recites the creed, prays and does good deeds, but neglects zakat, there will be no salvation. There is a reciprocal relationship between the practice of zakat and experiencing God's mercy (Caner 2002).

Judaism

"There is a time to act," says Ecclesiastes. For Jews, the deed is more important than the thought. Who we are is equal to what we do. Making amends heals us and the world; we begin to actively restore shalom, unity, and wholeness to the world (Olitsky 1991).

Native American Spirituality

As we walk on the path of forgiveness and justice, we stay focused on the things we have done wrong. We are on the path to becoming right with the Creator and with others (White Bison 2002).

Taoism

The twenty-seventh verse asks us to give to others without keeping an account or expecting something in return. This principle equates giving with receiving. One is equally as important and virtuous as the other. Both are equal aspects of the practice of circulation. Both require an element of trust – trust that ultimately, justice and fairness prevail. Trust in the law of karma, which affirms that for every action, there is a corresponding reaction. When we learn to trust in the Tao, we come to understand that everything exists in harmony. Nature is harmony. In order for us to live harmoniously, we need to give whenever possible and to receive whatever is given (Dyer 2007).

Step 10: Continued to take personal inventory and when we were wrong, promptly admitted it.

> **Definition:** to stand firm; steadfastness; endurance; continued pursuit, continuance

Perseverance—the Tenth Unifying Principle of the Twelve Wisdom Steps

Most of us recognize the common definition of perseverance, which is persistence in any activity we have undertaken, or continuation of something we have begun.

There is also a theological definition we may not be aware of, which undergirds the spirit of this step – "continuation in a state of grace." Working these steps and committing to this dedicated practice ensures the quality of our spirituality and continuance in the state of the grace. It corresponds with being given a "warranty" or "guarantee" as the result of one's continued practice. What a gift!

Christianity is much like the Twelve Steps. It places the responsibility of our spiritual health on our daily praxis and defines the key practices as examination, repentance, confession, forgiveness, and restitution. Corrective action should be made within twenty-four hours. Judaism also requires a daily mitzvah of taking inventory and making amends.

Each of the wisdom traditions bases spiritual progress on following prescribed steps – whether it be the Five Precepts of Buddhism, the cycle of birth and rebirth in Hinduism until knowledge replaces ignorance; or repentance in Islam, which is required in order to receive divine mercy and forgiveness.

The underlying message of all these traditions is that man can't figure it out alone – that salvation or enlightenment is dependent on following set prescribed practices, some of which must be dutifully observed on a daily basis. And when this commitment is made and followed diligently, we are blessed with a "continued state of grace."

Buddhism

The Five Precepts are the five categories of action from which everyone should abstain (much like the Ten Commandments). The difference is, in Buddhism, there is no final authority who judges our actions and doles out rewards or punishment. In Buddhism, everyone has the right to voluntarily choose to live by these Precepts out of compassion for themselves and for all sentient beings on Earth. When we live by these Precepts, we ensure all creatures absolute safety and we know we cannot create negative karma (Gerhards 2007).

Christianity

Even though we strive to be Christ like, at times we fail. Our conversion is a lifelong process. We are responsible for the maintenance of our spiritual state of being, which requires daily examination, repentance, confession, forgiveness, and restitution. If we err, we need to address it immediately (within twenty-four hours is a good rule of thumb). It is a simple, easy practice that allows us to keep our side of the street clean in all relationships. This practice of righting our wrongs daily results in true and lasting change, from who we were to who we want to become (Monahan 2001).

Cosmology

For Earth and its species to continue to evolve on its trajectory of growth and bountifulness, it is imperative we come to understand our proper place in the universal scheme. The time is now for us to take responsibility for our choices and actions because we are interconnected with all beings. We need to recognize our strengths, gifts and assets, as well as our limitations and challenges. We need to make a concerted and committed effort daily to walk this Earth in integrity (Dowd 2008).

Hinduism

Samsara is the endless round of rebirth from which Hindus seek to be free. The spiritual self lives on and will be held accountable for all the choices made. When we pass on to the next world for judgment, Yama tallies the soul's record and determines whether we receive reward or punishment. The sinless are led to the paradise of Brahma and the less virtuous will return to embody life at a higher level than the last. Death and judgment occur as often as each soul needs until it achieves freedom from rebirth. In the fourth Teaching of the Gita, Krishna tells Arjuna, in very clear terms, to follow his ways and be purified through the fire of knowledge. Knowledge will replace ignorance and free him from the cycle of samsara (Viswanathan 1992).

Islam

Islam requires true repentance in order to receive divine mercy, forgiveness, and eternal salvation (Caner 2002).

Judaism

In Judaism, there is a tradition to arise early to do a mitzvah. As a result, your entire day will be more tranquil. Jews are expected to take inventory and make amends. The Jewish tradition teaches that we are not required to finish the work, but neither are we free to desist from it. The inventory and the action to correct any wrongdoing become one and the same, simultaneously (Olitsky 1991).

Native American Spirituality

This step is about moment-to-moment inner alertness and offering instant amends when necessary. The only way to change old habits is to create new ones. When we practice being a positive warrior, the negative warrior eventually fades into the background. If we are consistent and diligent, we make a new life (White Bison 2002).

Taoism

"Be poised and centered in the midst of all activities." The twenty-sixth verse of the *Tao Te Ching* advises us how to maintain serenity in the midst of any circumstance. The source of this serenity comes from within and is, therefore, always available. The essence of the truth in this verse is that circumstances don't determine our emotions and actions unless we allow them; the power of choice resides within us. The challenge is always to maintain a state of stillness and calm, even in the midst of chaos. This paradoxical balance is symbolized by the opposing energies of the yin and yang. This practice will develop the skills of self-mastery within us. The Tao states that when we allow ourselves to be "blown to and fro" by the changing circumstances in our lives, we are no longer centered by our roots, and we become restless and vulnerable (Mitchell 1988).

Step 11: Sought through prayer and meditation to improve our conscious contact with God as we understood Him, praying only for knowledge of His will for us and the power to carry that out.

> **Definition:** Meditation is a disciplined practice in which the mind is focused on an object or the awareness of itself. It requires focusing attention on a single point of reference. The practice often results in the experience of a higher state of consciousness. It has been practiced for over 5,000 years and is present in most faith traditions.

Spirituality—the Eleventh Unifying Principle of the Twelve Wisdom Steps

Spirituality is the result of using prayer and meditation as techniques to "improve our conscious contact with God as we understand Him/Her/It." A key operative word in this explanation is "conscious," which is defined as knowledge, sensitivity to or awareness. A second operative word is "understand," which means: comprehension of, or the ability to grasp the idea of something. And third is "contact," which means to touch, to meet or a union. All of these definitions speak directly to this being a "process," much like any relationship. It takes time to get to know someone, to develop common language and understanding, and to maintain and grow the relationship requires a desire, commitment, work and, oftentimes, learning new skills. This step spells out the skills needed: prayer and meditation.

Prayer is integral to most traditions. It takes many forms, including supplication, worship, veneration, petition, confession, and thanksgiving. Prayer can be delivered publicly, in private, or written. Many people are most comfortable repeating written prayers, which are passed down from generation to generation through religions and cultures. Others prefer a more conversational approach and "dialogue," as if talking to a kind, interested listener who may or may not be influenced in how they use their power. It has often been said that prayer is our side of the conversation, and we receive our answers through meditation, inspiration, and spiritual messages we encounter in church services and spiritual reading.

In Islam, prayer is a commitment of faith. Muslims are called to prayer five times daily. This time is dedicated to expressing their faithfulness to God and reminding them of the commitment to His way of life.

Meditation is a disciplined practice in which the mind is focused on an object or the awareness of itself, or, frequently, on the breath. It requires focusing one's attention to a single point of reference. The practice often produces a higher state of consciousness. It has been practiced for over 5,000 years and is found in many faith traditions.

The purpose of meditation in Buddhism is to clear and transform the mind. Mindfulness is being aware of the conditions of the mind (of your thoughts). In Buddhism, we learn there is an "observer" which can step aside and observe both our thoughts and our actions. There is a full range of conditions, which can be experienced by the mind, from serenity through fear and anxiety to the bliss of Nirvana. For anyone to become fully awakened, they must learn the art and practice of mindfulness both during meditation and during normal day-to-day activities. Mindfulness keeps us in touch with ourselves and with the present moment. It provides the opportunity to make choices: changing our thinking, letting go of negative thoughts, and selecting actions from a range of options. With practice, mindfulness becomes a way of living.

Buddhism

The primary function of Buddhist meditation is to transform the mind. Mindfulness is being aware of the conditions of the mind (of your thoughts). In Buddhism, we learn there is an "observer" which can step aside and observe both our thoughts and our actions. There is a full range of conditions, which can be experienced by the mind from serenity through fear and anxiety to the bliss of Nirvana. For anyone to become fully awakened, he or she must learn the art and practice of mindfulness, both during meditation and during normal day-to-day activities. Mindfulness keeps us in touch with ourselves and with the present moment.

It provides the opportunity to make choices: changing our thinking, letting go of negative thoughts, and selecting actions from a range of options. With practice, mindfulness becomes a way of living (Griffin 2004).

Christianity

For most Christians, our goal is to become more Christ-like. In order to do so, we require wisdom and direction. We are encouraged to develop a personal relationship with Christ so that we are available to learn and be directed. This relationship grows and matures through our ability to talk, to listen, and to follow Divine guidance. It has often been said that prayer is our side of the conversation, and meditation is the time to listen. Often, the responses come through inspiration, through spiritual messages in books and church services, through opportunities that present themselves synchronistically. Part of our responsibility is to stay open, awake, and aware (Selby 2000).

Cosmology

Spirituality provides a way for us to remember who we are and to reconnect with our Source. It teaches us how to build relationship with the Originating Mystery (LaChance 1991).

Hinduism

Meditation is necessary for the mystical insight that alone could be the cause of liberation. Meditation firmly secures knowledge already gained. It is necessary for liberation. It prepares the person for the emergence of inner knowledge. The person who has realized the Self has transcended desire, lacking nothing and being free from compulsions. Because karma can interfere with the constant remembrance of Brahman, meditation is necessary (Viswanathan 1992).

Islam

Prayer is called five times daily, and devout Muslims stop and pray at these times. The prayer leader (muezzin) chants the Call to Prayer in Arabic. Muslims pray to express their faithfulness to God and remind themselves of their devotion to Him and to His way of life. Prayer is a commitment of faith; it removes evil and prepares one for final rewards in Heaven (Caner 2002).

Judaism

Judaism teaches we can come into contact with God through any activity with the right intention. God is present in all things and in all people so we can come into conscious contact with God through any of our interactions with the world. Through these interactions, we become aware of God's presence in our lives (Olitsky 1991).

Native American Spirituality

We have always been a people of prayer. Something inside us becomes alert when an elder prays. This step is about reawakening our gift of prayer and using it for recovery. Many of us view a path as a narrow trail, but a spiritual path is unlimited. Prayer and meditation widen the path and remove obstacles in our way. When we seek something bigger than our ego-self, we find self-esteem. The deep root of our wellness is our relationship with the Great Mystery. Prayer and meditation keep our spiritual awareness of the unseen world of Spirit very close (White Bison 2002).

Taoism

The *Tao Te Ching* describes itself as invisible, inaudible, and intangible. Yet through our intuition, we can see, hear, and feel it as one presence. It is not something we can grasp and hold, but rather, something that we can learn to be; and when we have some mastery in the practice, we will experience "ease" in our life: tranquility, serenity, harmony, and freedom from suffering (Dyer 2007).

Step 12: Having had a spiritual awakening as the result of these steps, we tried to carry the message to others, and to practice these principles in all our affairs.

Definition: an act, which is performed without any expectation of result or award for the person performing it.

Service—the Twelfth Unifying Principle of the Twelve Wisdom Steps

Service is defined as the performance of labor for the benefit of another. It is derived from the Latin word *sevare*, which means to protect or preserve. There are many applications of this interpretation; the most obvious one being the protection of the spiritual principles and practices of these Steps by gifting them to others; inherent in this interpretation is the labor of love that in the end benefits others, as well as self. The by-product of this individual giving of self to another is community building, the shared experiences which create a common bond.

In cosmology, we find that communion or interrelationship is the underlying principle of the universe. It has been called "common-unity." Everything in the universe is in communion with everything else. It is all interdependent and interrelated in an unbroken bond of connectivity. There is no separation – diversity and subjectivity yes, but no separateness. When we come to understand our "oneness," it is so much easier to care for, accept, support, and empathize with others.

The sense of solidarity shared by Muslims is highly valued. They view themselves as a community (umma) who share their belief in Allah. They value their spiritual kinship and their own individual freedom.

Christ provided an ideal blueprint. He told his disciples we are intended to carry forth His ministry. "You are the light of the world." When we live these Twelve Steps, our actions will speak louder than our words. They guide us in the demonstration of a Christ-like life. It is only when we are in service that we are able to share with others the many gifts we have received.

Buddhism

During his life, the Buddha taught and ordained disciples who became known as the *Sangha*. The primary purpose of the Sangha was (and is) to continue to teach the precepts. The Sangha is considered to be one of the Three Refuges or jewels of Buddhism. It is respected as a community of noble beings who have realized at least one of the four stages on the Buddhist path to spirituality. When someone takes refuge in the Sangha, they are actually relying on one of these noble beings for guidance, much like a new member in A.A. relies on a sponsor to guide them through the Steps and support them as they practice their new way of living (Ash 1993).

Christianity

Christ prepared the Way. He created the ideal blueprint of how to live a Christ-like life. He told us that He and the Father are one and that we, too, can have this same relationship manifested in our lives when we reach out and love our neighbors as ourselves. In fact, we are intended to carry forth His ministry. He told us with great clarity, "You are the light of the world." When we live these Twelve Steps as they are laid out, our actions will speak louder than our words. They guide us in the demonstration of a Christ-like life. It is only when we are in service to others that we are able to give to others the many gifts we have received (Monahan 2001.

Cosmology

Communion or interrelationship is the underlying principle of the universe. Everything in the universe is in communion with everything else. It is interdependent and interrelated in an unbroken bond of connectivity. There is no separation – diversity and subjectivity yes, but no separateness (Berry 2000).

Hinduism

The mind's capacity (*samarthyam*) to carry out its function is contingent on illumination provided by the infinite and unconditioned light of consciousness. Brahman is the light of consciousness. Karma yoga is the performance of an action with detachment from the results for the sake of worshipping the Lord (*isvararadhanarthe*). It is action performed in a spirit of selfless sacrifice to God (Viswanathan 1992).

Islam

The sense of solidarity shared by Muslims is highly valued. They view themselves as a community (*umma*) who share their belief in Allah. They value their spiritual kinship and their own in-

dividual freedom. The pilgrimage to Mecca (Hajj), has the ultimate benefit of the pilgrim receiving forgiveness for sins. The
actual events heighten one's God consciousness and create a sense
of spiritual fulfillment. Muhammad promised that those who perform the Hajj would return from it as a "newly-born baby," im-
plying a freedom from sin. It also encompasses the three main
practices necessary to achieve eternal salvation: hard work, prayer,
and forgiveness from sin from Allah (Caner 2002).

Judaism

As the result of these steps, your Judaism has been renewed.
Continue to work them again and again. Just as each Passover
we are back in Egypt again as slaves, so each time we rework a
step, we confront the addiction anew. It is important to concen-
trate on your own practice before carrying the message to others.
From Pirke Avot 4:5 - "Regarding the person who learns in order
to teach, Heaven will allow that person to continue to learn and
to teach. But concerning the one who learns in order to practice,
Heaven allows that person to learn and to teach, observe and
practice," (Olitsky 1991).

Native American Spirituality

As individuals, we can help our brothers and sisters who are
still suffering from drug and alcohol abuse one-on-one. We can
talk to them about what our lives were like, about the journey
we took to heal ourselves, about what we are like now, and our
vision for the future. We can share the good that happened to us
when we began to walk the Red Road by blending the Medicine
Wheel Teachings of our traditions with the Twelve Steps of A.A.
We have had spiritual experiences, and we found that the vision
we created through our mind maps are now coming true in the
Twelfth Step (White Bison 2002).

Taoism

The secret of the Tao is in serving. The reason that both
heaven and earth last forever is because they do not live for themselves, but for others. It is a simple message and formula for happiness. The seventh verse affirms the law of circulation – by

giving without expectation, everything we need will be provided. "Serve the needs of others, and all your own needs will be fulfilled." The Tao describes the perpetual and eternal free-flowing power from the Source, which sustains and endures. Our work is to understand that we are one with this power, which flows through, and as us, when we are willing and available (Mitchell 1988).

Chapter Six

Personal Reflections

It has been a two-and-a-half year journey since I began the actual hands on work of researching the texts and writings of the wisdom traditions to discover if, in fact, the underlying principles of these traditions are universal. It is opportune to take a retrospective mountaintop view of the road on which I have been traveling. It provides an opportunity to recognize the curves in the road, which contributed unexpected lessons and gifts. As a woman, the closest comparison is to gestation and birthing. Not being an "artist" who has created something from nothing (particularly of this magnitude) which is the result of a "form" in one's mind's eye – this is the closest resemblance.

What first comes to mind is how this project's creative process is the affirmation of core spiritual beliefs I hold which have been evidenced multi-fold over the many years of my life. When I was obtaining my master's degree in communications (rhetorical) in the 1980s, I delved into the relationship between Platonic Ideas and Noam Chomsky's thesis that all people across cultures are born with apriori language forms, which, in its rudiments, points to a collective unconscious. Plato's theory of idealism is based on universals or abstract forms that are often described as "thoughts in the mind" (of God or a universal intelligence). The idea is both abstract and universal; the form is both particularized and concrete.

:her clarification of the word "universal" means those
that share similar characteristics or qualities; they are re-
.t. The universal form has many particularizations. The example frequently used is the concept of "redness" which does not
exist unless it is particularized as a characteristic of "things."

Noam Chomsky, an American linguist and philosopher, applied Plato's theory to language. His theory is based on a 'universal' grammar or set of linguistic principles shared by all
languages. He refers to them as linguistic universals.

Carl Jung, renowned Swiss psychiatrist and analytical psychologist, developed a concept of the "collective unconscious,"
which is the locus of all accumulated archetypal experience and is
accessed by the deepest level of the human psyche or consciousness, which is the source of creativity, inspiration, and new ideas.
In vernacular terms, it is the "treasure trove" of all prototypes (or
Ideas), which are the "forms" that are eternally copied, patterned,
and emulated. These "Ideas" or "forms" are also known as "universal symbols."

It is no wonder I migrated from being a Unitarian
Universalist to a New Thought Religious Scientist. The twenty-
five years of grounding in Unitarianism deepened and integrated
my philosophical beginnings founded in Emerson, Thoreau, and
the Transcendentalists when I was in high school. Unitarian
Universalists are so named because they do not subscribe to a
creed; they are unified by their shared search for Truth. They in-
vestigate all religions and traditions and explore their diverse practices. They honor and value aspects of all religions, and appreciate
the universality they represent in the world. The extent to which
the elements of any particular faith tradition are incorporated into
one's personal spiritual practices is a matter of personal choice.

New Thought, which is closely associated with Religious
Science, is not based on any "authority" of established beliefs,
but rather on "what it can accomplish" for those who practice it.
It promotes the ideas that "Infinite Intelligence" or "God" is
ubiquitous, that Spirit is the totality of all things (both imma-
nent and transcendent); that human Selfhood is divine; that
divine thought is only good, and "right thinking" has a healing
effect. New Thought holds true that God is "Infinite Intelligence"

which is universal, that it dwells within each person. It also follows Teilhard de Chardin's (a Jesuit priest and theologian) belief that people are "spiritual beings having a human experience." A key belief is that one's thoughts are manifested into reality and become our life experience. When I transitioned to New Thought in 1999, it jump-started my deeper spiritual inquiry. Over the next ten years, I became a chaplain, studied two years at an interfaith seminary, and six years at Wisdom University along with a disciplined daily spiritual practice.

Religious Science teaches that all beings are expressions of, and part of, Infinite Intelligence (or God). Because this Infinite Intelligence is all there is, its power can be accessed by all humans if, through spiritual practice(s), they align themselves with its presence. Ernest Holmes said "God is not...a person, but Universal Presence...already in our own soul, already operating through our own consciousness," (Vahle 1993).

The next step in the evolution of this spiritual growth training was to understand the application of these principles in my life. As Holmes described, it is based on people's ability to "align themselves with its presence through spiritual practice." One of the primary tasks of spiritual practice is to practice learning to become still in order to connect with oneself and with one's Creator, and to realize God or Source or Infinite Intelligence (or whatever one names it) as the first, primal, and ultimate Creative force. When I grasped this, I integrated the Jewish belief that God is a verb, an evolutionary process, without end. This means, every moment new life is being created, and existing life is being transformed. We are a process; all existence is a process. We, as humans, are in the process of be-coming; of increasing our awareness, of gaining new insights, of shifting our thinking and our behaviors. This dynamic change process begins with awareness and thought. We are co-creators with the Creative Power. Ernest Holmes explained,

"Within us there is a creative field, which we call subjective mind; around us there is a creative field which we call Subjective. One is universal and the other is individual, but in reality they are one...the individual mind is really not individual but is individualized. Behind the individual is the universal, which has no limits.... Everyone is universal on the subjective side of life, and individual only at the point of conscious perception....we all use the creative power of the Universal Mind every time we use our own mind. All thought therefore is creative," (Holmes 1997).

The Kabbalah also affirms that creation is a thought in the mind of God. The Kabbalah states, "Will, which is primordial thought, is the beginning of all things, and the expression (of this thought) is the completion," (Zohar 1983). This quote from the ancient Jewish tradition implies creation is nothing more than thought in the mind. And thought is connected to will, or intention. Every human has free will and the Jewish belief is that at the core of free will, is the will to give, which is the "Godness" in each of us.

"The human capacity of acting like God in being a bestower is the fulcrum upon which the entire universe is balanced," (Cooper 1997).

Free will is fundamental to Judaism, because if humans only had the capacity to 'receive,' then life would be predetermined. The capacity of free will to 'give' allows creation to unfold as it is willed. And what is will? It is the human capacity to form an intention, to make a decision, to manifest something. It is the form through which thought and energy manifest an outcome. It is this capacity that allows humans to co-create with the Creator.

The following chart is my personal attempt to reconcile the triune (Trinitarian view of God) with the unity (Unitarian) concept of Oneness. The first column is God: the Source, the thought, the idea, the Creator, the beginning of the beginning. The second column is the subjective substance: the substance on, or through, which the thought, the idea, the intention passes through in order to be created or manifested. And the third column is what is manifested: the effect, the physical, the form, the experience, that which is created. At a metaphysical level, God is the Creator, and when our soul becomes aware of or is conscious of its relationship or oneness with God, then it also becomes aware of its ability to co-create —being proactive rather than reactive. This process is an awareness and recognition of our own potentiality, which, in combination with intention and/or energy, allows us to co-create or manifest our own experience. This occurs for us much as the potential of an oak tree lies within the seeds of the acorn.

Spirit/God	Mind	Body
Metaphysical	Nonphysical	Physical
Thought	Energy	Manifestation
Conscious	Subconscious	Unconscious
Cause	Medium	Effect
Seed	Soil	Plant
Thought (vibration)	Substance	Form
Idea/Thought	Paint	Painting
Intention	Law	Manifestation
Thought	Word (symbols/language)	Experience
Knowing	Tao	Doing
Creator	Soul	Co-creator
Knowing (God the Father)	Being (the Holy Spirit)	Experiencing (God the Son)
Either	Energy	Matter

Figure 11. Trinitarian view of Creative Source

In returning to my retrospective mountaintop view of this journey, I believe the www.12wisdomsteps.com interactive project is a particularized manifestation of my own thought forms, reflecting an emanation of universal, archetypal Ideas, which underlie not only these eight wisdom traditions, but the evolutionary, spiritual emergent process of humans as they transgress from earlier Darwinian-defined homo erectus to a futurist homo spiritus.

I can reflect on my own simple evolutionary process, which began with Alfred North Whitehead, English mathematician and philosopher, and the American Transcendentalists at age sixteen to the culmination of my spiritual progress to date. Whitehead implanted in me the first seeds of a universe characterized by process and change, the results of which are particularized by the free-will choices and decisions we make. He believed that self-determination characterizes everything in the universe, not just human beings. In Ralph Waldo Emerson's essay, *"The American Scholar,"* he called for a revolution in human consciousness, "to build, therefore, your own world. As fast as you conform your life to the pure idea in your mind, that will unfold its great proportions. A correspondent revolution in things will attend the influx of the spirit (Emerson 1842). As noted earlier in this section, these formative beliefs were followed and further entrenched by Plato's Universal Ideas and Noam Chomsky's universal language, which I studied for my master's degree.

The Unitarian Universalists then provided permission (for twenty-five years) to seek the Truth (Universal Truths) in all religions/traditions and to explore their practices. New Thought and Religious Science contributed a comprehensive understanding of Universal Intelligence and the application of co-creativity using spiritual practices in combination with accessing the Universal Intelligence. During this period, I became immersed in the Twelve-Step model of ethical living and cognitive behavioral therapy, which focuses on changing one's thinking in order to change one's experience. Two years of interfaith studies at One Spirit provided an introduction to the principles, beliefs, texts, and practices of the major faith traditions. My studies at Wisdom University have stretched the edges of my knowing in so many areas: cosmology and the interconnectedness of the universe; the merging of energy and mystical gnosis in quantum theology; Creation Spirituality's paradigm of human existence; the journey from mysticism (Howard Thurman) to activism (Martin Luther King, Gandhi and Andrew Harvey); the essence of harmony, balance, and Spirit through Shintoism in Japan; and applied wisdom from the ages in Wisdom and Civilization. All of this has shaped the spiritual foundation nurturing the creative thought form, "12wisdomsteps.com" to emerge from the unknown (collective unconscious) to the known (my conscious) into its particularized form.

And in this particularized dimension (my everyday life), there is much formative experience that contributed to this emergent project. Other aspects of my life experience that have contributed to this creative process include journalism (investigative mind; inquiry; writing skills); advertising (visual layout and design); photography (visual composition, balance and harmony); accounting (linear thinking, recording, classifying and summarizing data); systems design (systems theory); teaching (transmitting and translating knowledge designed to reach a specific audience); cognitive behavioral therapy (assisting others in reframing their thinking and behaviors), and, interfaith ministry (supporting others in their path of self discovery of truth and meaning).

This retrospective mountaintop view has led me to understand how www.12wisdomsteps.com is the culmination at this juncture of my spiritual evolution, life experiences, and the knowledge, wisdom, and skills acquired on the journey.

And when I consider the product of this journey and personalize its meaning, I must admit that when I go to bed at the end of the day, I am awed and grateful to learn that someone like the individual(s) in the Russian Federation, viewed nineteen pages on www.12wisdomsteps.com while I was sleeping, and hopefully found deeper meaning, trust in something greater and a more committed life purpose.

Appendix A

Spiritual Practices and Facilitator's Workbook
Accompanies interactive website
www.12wisdomsteps.com

To provide website users with additional tools and practices to enhance their spirituality, either in their own wisdom tradition, or to begin immersing themselves in another, this writer compiled groups of practices from each faith tradition into a manual which can be downloaded or ordered on the website. It includes a helpful guide that provides steps on how to develop a daily spiritual practice.

For those who work in the social services field using spiritual tools, practices, and the Twelve Steps, each Step Chapter includes a list of facilitator questions that can be used in various group settings to promote self-discovery and discussion.

Literature Review and Bibliography

Alcoholics Anonymous Preamble. *A.A. Grapevine*, 1947.

Alcoholics Anonymous. New York: A.A. World Services, Inc. 1976

Arberry, Arthur J. trans. *The Koran Interpreted*. New York: Macmillan Pub. Co., 1986.

Armstrong, K. "Compassion is the Key." *Resurgence* 235 (March/April 2006).

Ash, Mel. *The Zen of Recovery*. New York: Penguin Putnam, Inc., 1993.

Babbitt, Irving. *Translation of Dhammapada*. New York: New Directions, 1965.

Bennet, Sage. *Wisdom Walk: Nine Practices for Creating Peace and Balance from the World's Spiritual Traditions*. Novato Calif.: New World Library, 2007.

Berry, Thomas. *The Dream of the Earth*. San Francisco: Sierra Club Books, 1988.

—. *The Great Work: Our Way into the Future*. 1st ed. New York: Bell Tower, 2000.

—. *The Sacred Universe: Earth, Spirituality, and Religion in the Twenty-First Century*. New York: Columbia University Press, 2009.

Brown, Joseph Epes. *The Sacred Pipe*. Baltimore: Penguin, 1971.

Caner, Ergun. *Unveiling Islam: An Insider's Look at Muslim Life and Beliefs*. Grand Rapids MI: Kregel Publications, 2002.

Chang, Stephen. *The Complete System of Self-Healing: Internal Exercises*. San Francisco CA.: Tao Pub., 1986.

Cheever, Susan. *My Name is Bill.*(New York: Simon & Schuster, 2004.

Cleary. T. *The Essential Koran*. San Franciso: HarperSanFrancisco, 1993.

Cook, M. *The Koran: A Very Short Introduction*. Oxford, UK: Oxford UP, 2000.

Cooper, David A. *God is a Verb*. New York: Penguin Putnam, 1997.

Dahlke, Rudiger. *Mandalas of the World*. New York: Sterling Publishing Co., Inc. 1992.

Dawood, N.J. *The Koran*. London and New York: Penguin, 1956; reprint, 1990. Translation.

Dick, B. *The Good Book and the Big Book: A.A.'s Roots in the Bible*. Bridge builders ed. Kihei Hawaii: Paradise Research Publications, 1997.

Dowd, Michael. *Thank God for Evolution: How the Marriage of Science and Religion will Transform your Life and Our World*. 1st ed. New York: Viking, 2008.

Dyer, Dr. Wayne D. *Change Your Thoughts - Change Your Life, Living the Wisdom of the Tao*. Carlsbad, CA: Hay House, 2007.

Eliot. *Japanese Buddhism*. London: 1935

Emerson, Ralph Waldo. "The Transcendentalist." (Lecture, Masonic Temple, Boston, MA, January, 1842.)

Esposito, John L. *What Everyone Needs to Know about Islam*. Oxford University Press, 2002.

Exploring Deep Ecology. Discussion Course. Portland, OR: Northwest Earth Institute, 2001.

Fanning, Patrick. *The Addiction Workbook: A Step-by-Step Guide to Quitting Alcohol & Drugs*. Oakland CA: New Harbinger Publications, 1996.

Fischer-Schreiber, Ingrid. *The Encyclopedia of Eastern philosophy and Religion: Buddhism, Hinduism, Taoism, Zen*. Boston: Shambhala, 1994.

Foster, Richard. *Celebration of Discipline: The Path to Spiritual Growth*. 1st ed. San Francisco: Harper & Row, 1988.

Fox, Emmet. *The Sermon on the Mount*. San Francisco: Harper Collins, 1989.

Gerhards, Paul. *Mapping the Dharma*. Vancouver, WA: Parmi Press, 2007.

Griffin, Kevin. *One Breath at a Time*: *Buddhism and he Twelve Steps* www.rodalestore.com, 2004.

Gorski, Terence, and Alcoholics Anonymous. *Understanding the Twelve Steps: A Guide for Counselors, Therapists, and Recovering People*. Independence Mo.: Herald House/Independence Press, 1989.

Hammond, Lisa, and Gorski, Terence. *Working the Program*. Independence, MO: Herald House/Independence Press, 2005.

Harvey, Peter. *An Introduction to Buddhism: Teachings, History and Practices*. Cambridge University Press, 1990.

Hawley, Jack. *The Bhagavad Gita, A Walkthrough for Westerners*. Novato, CA: New World Library, 2001.

Hazelden. *A Program for You: Guide to the Big Book's Design for Living*. Center City: Hazelden, 1991.

Heinze, Andrew R. "The Americanization of Mussar: Abraham Twerski's Twelve Steps*.*" *Judaism* (Fall 1999).

Holmes,Ernest. *The Science of Mind*. New York: Penguin Putnam, 1997.

Hooper, Richard. *Jesus, Buddha, Krishna, Lao Tzu The Parallel Sayings*. Sedona, AZ: Sanctuary Publications, Inc., 2007.

Hughes, Kerry. *The Incense Bible: Plant Scents that Transcend World Culture, Medicine, and Spirituality*. New York: Hayworth Press, 2007.

Humphreys, R..H. Moos, and C. Cohen. "Social and Community Resources and Long-term Recovery from Treated and Untreated Alcoholism." *Journal of Studies on Alcohol* 58 (1997): 231-8.

Ingerman, Sandra. *How to Heal Toxic Thoughts*. New York: Sterling Pub. Co., 2007.

James, William. *Varieties of Religious Experience*. New York: Simon & Schuster, Inc., 1997.

Jantsch, Erich. *The Self-Organizing Universe*. New York: Pergamon Books, 1980.

Kelly, John F., Stout, Robert, Magill, Molly, Tonigan, J. Scott, Pagano, Maria E. "Mechanisms of behavior change in alcoholics anonymous: does Alcoholics Anonymous lead to better alcohol use outcomes by reducing depression symptoms?" *Addiction*. http://psychservices.psychiatryonline.org/cgi/content/full/57/12/1758 (accessed Jan. 22, 2010 3:58AM)

Kim, Ha Poong. *Reading Lao Tzu: A Companion to the Tao Te Ching With a New Translation*. Xlibris Corporation, 2003.

Kornfield, Jack. *After the Ecstasy, the Laundry: How the Heart Grows Wise on the Spiritual Path*. New York: Bantam Books, 2000.

Kurtz, Ernest. *Not-God: A History of Alcoholics Anonymous*. Center City, MN: Hazelden, 1979.

—*The Spirituality of Imperfection: Storytelling and the Journey to Wholeness*. New York: Bantam, 1994.

LaChance, Albert. *Greenspirit: Twelve Steps in Ecological Spirituality, an Individual, Cultural, and Planetary Therapy*. Rockport Mass.: Element, 1991.

—*The Architecture of the Soul: A Unitive Model of the Human Person*. Berkeley Calif.: North Atlantic Books, 2006.

Lovelock, James. *The Ages of Gaia*. New York: Norton & Co. 1985.

Matt, Daniel. *The Essential Kabbalah: The Heart of Jewish Mysticism*. New York: Quality Paperback Book Club, 1998.

McDowell, Robert. Poetry as Spiritual Practice: *Reading, Writing, and Using Poetry in Your Daily Rituals, Aspirations, and Intentions*. 1st ed. New York: Free Press, 2008.

McGregor, Jim. *The Tao of Recovery: A Quiet Path to Wholeness*. New York: Bantam Books, 1992.

Medicine Wheel and the 12 Steps for Men. Medicine Wheel and the 12 Steps for Women. www.whitebison.org.

Miller, John. *God's Breath: Sacred Scriptures of the World*. New York: Marlowe & Co., 2000.

Mitchell, Stephen. Translation. *Tao Te Ching*. San Francisco: Harper & Row, 1988.

Monahan, Sister Molly. *Seeds of Grace: Reflections on the Spirituality of Alcoholics Anonymous*. New York: Riverhead Books, 2001.

Narcotics Anonymous. The Narcotics Anonymous Step Working Guides. Chatsworth CA: Narcotics Anonymous World Services, 1998.

Neihardt, John G. *Black Elk Speaks*. New York: Washington Square Press. 1959.

Nigosian, S.A. *Islam: Its History, Teaching and Practices*. Bloomington: Indiana: University Press, 2004.

Novak, Philip. *The World's Wisdom*. San Francisco: Harper Collins, 1995.

Nowinski, Joseph. *The Twelve-Step Facilitation Handbook: A Systematic Approach to early Recovery from Substance Dependence*. Center City Minn.: Hazelden, 2003.

Olitzky, Rabbi Kerry M. & Copans, Stuard A. *Twelve Jewish Steps to Recovery*. Woodstock, Vermont: Jewish Lights Publishing, 1991.

NSRV: *The Bible: New Revised Standard Version*. London and New York: Collins, 1989.

Perry, Whitall. *The Spiritual Ascent: A Compendium of the World's Wisdom*. Louisville KY: Fons Vitae, 2007.

Prabhavananda, Swami and Isherwood, Christopher. trans. *Bhagavad Gita*. New York: New American Library. 1944.

Practice these principles and What is the Oxford Group? Center City, MN: Hazelden, 1997.

Rahula, Walpola. *What the Buddha Taught*. New York: Grove Press, 1959.

Red Road to Wellbriety. White Bison, Inc. Colorado Springs, CO: White Bison, Inc., 2002.

Renard, John. *Responses to 101 Questions on Islam*. New York: Paulist Press, 1998.

Renard, John. *Responses to 101 Questions on Hinduism*. New York: Paulist Press, 1999.

Rieger, D.A. et al. "Co-morbidity of Mental Disorders with Alcohol and Other Drug Abuse: Results of the Environmental Catchment Area Study." *JAMA*, 264 (1990) 19: 2511-2518.

Ringwald, Christopher D. *The Soul of Recovery*. Oxford: Oxford University Press, 2002.

Rohr, Richard. *How Do We Breathe Under Water? The Gospel and 12-Step Spirituality*. Vol. 4.

S. Laura. 12 Steps on Buddha's Path. Boston: Wisdom Publications, 2006.

Satchidananda, Sri Swami. *The Living Gita*. Yogaville, VA: Integral Yoga Publications, 1988.

Schlitz, Marilyn. *Living Deeply: The Art & Science of Transformation in Everyday Life*. Oakland CA: New Harbinger Publications, 2007.

Schut, Michael. *Simpler Living Compassionate Life: A Christian Perspective*. Denver CO: Living the Good News, 1999.

Selby, John. *Seven Masters, One Path: Meditation Secrets from the World's Greatest Teachers*. 1st ed. San Francisco: Harper San Francisco, 2003.

Selby, Saul. *Twelve Step Christianity: The Christian Roots and Application of the Twelve Steps*. Center City MN.: Hazelden Information & Educational Services, 2000.

Seppala, Marvin D. *Clinicians Guide to The Twelve Step Principles*. New York: McGraw-Hill, 2001.

Shapiro, Dr. Philip. *Healing Power: Ten Steps to Pain Management and Spiritual Evolution*. Bloomington, IN: Authorhouse, 2005.

Sifton, Elisabeth. *The Serenity Prayer: Faith and Politics in Times of Peace and War*. 1st ed. New York: Norton, 2003.

Smith, Huston. The Illustrated World's Religions: A Guide to our Wisdom Traditions. 1st ed. San Francisco: HarperSanFrancisco,1995.

Sogyal, Rinpoche. *The Tibetan Book of Living and Dying*. Partick Gaffney and Andrew Harvey eds. New York: Harper Collins, 1994.

Tenzin-Dolma, Lisa. *Healing Mandalas*. London:Duncan Baird Publishers, 2008.

The Twelve Steps and Twelve Traditions. New York: Alcoholics Anonymous World Services, Inc., 1988.

Twerski, Abraham J. *The Spiritual Self*. Minnesota: Hazelden, 2000.

Vahle,Neal. *Open at the top: The Life of Ernest Holmes*. Open View Press, 1993.

Vaillant, George E. *The Natural History of Alcoholism.* Cambridge, MA: Harvard University Press, 1976.

Viswanathan. Ed. *Am I a Hindu?* San Francisco: Halo Books, 1992.

Vivekananda, Swami. *Complete Works of Swami Vivekananda.* Calcutta: 1987.

Warder A.K. *Indian Buddhism.* 3rd edition, 2000.

Watts, Alan. *What is Tao.* Novato Calif.: New World Library, 2000.

White Bison. *The Red Road to Wellbriety in the Native American Way.* Colorado Springs Colo.: White Bison Inc., 2002.

Wilson, William G. "An Explanation of the 12 Steps of Alcoholics Anonymous." *N.Y. STATE JOURNAL OF MEDICINE* Vol. 44 (August 1944).

Wilson, William G. "Basic Concepts of Alcoholics Anonymous." *N.Y. STATE JOURNAL OF MEDICINE* Vol. 44 (August 1944).

Wilson, William G. "Alcoholics Anonymous Comes of Age." New York: Alcoholics Anonymous World Services, Inc., 1957.

Working the Twelve Steps. Center City MN: Hazelden, 1988.

Zohar: Book of Enlightenment. New York: Paulist Press, 1983.